60 DAYS TO CHANGE

A DAILY HOW-TO GUIDE WITH ACTIONABLE
TIPS FOR IMPROVING YOUR FINANCIAL LIFE

Peter Dunn

Channel V Books
New York

Channel V Books
New York

Interior and Cover Design: Raquel G. Richardson
Cover Photography: Dan Kraner

Published in the United States by Channel V Books,
a division of Channel V Media, New York, NY.
www.ChannelVBooks.com

Channel V Books and its logo are trademarks of Channel V Media.

ISBN 978-0-9824739-1-7

Library of Congress Control Number: 2009934968

Library of Congress subject headings:
Finance, Personal.
Finance, Personal—United States.
Investments.

PRINTED IN THE UNITED STATES OF AMERICA

10 9 8 7 6 5 4 3 2 1

First Edition

Contents

Week Three: Control Monthly Spending

Week Four: Budget Week

Week Five: Risk Management

Week Six: Employee Benefits and Your Career

Week Seven: Develop Savings Habits

Week Eight: Major Purchases

Week Nine: Devise a Permanent Plan for Success

Introduction

I've always been a bit disappointed by the genesis of my first book, *What Your Dad Never Taught You About Budgeting*, because my inspiration for it was so superficial. (Yes, this introduction doubles as a confession, but at least I'm deep enough to admit it.)

It all started on a two-hour flight from Indianapolis to Houston when the very talkative (and very sweaty) Ron sat down next to me. Although I'd planned on relaxing by reading an issue of *Sports Illustrated*, I knew a magazine wasn't going to be enough to fend off Ron, who was already glancing over at me, looking for excuses to start a conversation. So, I popped open my laptop and started writing a book. And that's how my writing career began.

Like I said, I'm not proud of this, but I *am* proud of the groundwork I laid for my unique brand of financial advice during and after the writing process. Since the book's publication, I've launched my own radio show (*Skills Your Dad Never Taught You*) and hosted or been a guest on many others. I've appeared as a commentator on several national and local news shows, by-lined articles, participated in interviews for a number of respected publications and introduced GreenCandy.com, an online financial assessment tool for Gen Y-ers and Millennials.

I've even been seated next to many more talkative, sweaty guys on flights, yet I never felt compelled to start writing another book. Until now.

Why now? Well, I have a lot to say.

Over the last three years, I've noticed that people are chasing the American Dream with more determination than ever. But as they do, they're finding a path fraught with new peril, leading them—and the experts—to question the wisdom of this dream like never before. After all, despite the implicit— and explicit—cultural message that the dream is attainable for everyone, we've reached a time in our nation's history when many are asking hard questions: Does everyone deserve to live the American Dream or is it only for a select few? If so, for whom? Should everyone own a home? Should everyone retire with a gold watch? Is everyone entitled to a lazy retirement?

America is set up for success stories. Capitalism, the free-market system and a stable economy have always been the keystones of individual financial achievement. These keystones, however, have recently revealed their weaknesses. People continue to look for ways to succeed in spite of long-standing, challenging economic barriers to entry, and it is these people who are systematically redefining the terms of attaining the American Dream, for better or for worse. Well, for worse, really.

More than ever Americans are going after the American Dream at the expense of their financial futures. And a troubled national economy is only compounding individual financial troubles. The American Dream is beginning to feel like the American Nightmare.

But the economy will pick up and reinvent itself, and we need to achieve a sustainable American Dream the old-fashioned way: with hard work, financial know-how and commitment to setting and reaching our goals. If we can learn how to find financial success in an ugly economy, we'll no doubt flourish in a strong economy. And if we are able to set measurable benchmarks that allow us to live our own personal American Dreams, macro financial conditions should have significantly less impact on our micro financial lives.

This book is about setting both big and small financial goals, learning how to reach them and working hard to accomplish them. Your income is an incredibly powerful financial tool, and when you combine it with working knowledge of the financial world, you can create a great life for yourself. This book won't waste your time. It's a very concise blueprint for changing your financial life in just 60 days.

The same *60 Days to Change* curriculum that is presented in this book has already empowered thousands of people across the country. Multiple CBS and FOX affiliates featured the *60 Days to Change* program as a nine-week news series, and thousands of viewers signed up and followed along to improve their financial lives.

Now it's your turn.

Peter Dunn
a.k.a. "Pete the Planner"

Week One

You Don't Have to Be a Financial Genius to Be a Financial Success!

One of the most important things you'll learn over the next 60 days is that money really has very little to do with, well, money. In other words, your financial success will not rely primarily on what you've got in the bank but on your willingness to develop good financial habits. All too often people believe that to be a financial success you've got to be either a financial genius or born rich. *Please.* Financial success is attainable by anyone who's willing to eliminate bad habits and replace them with good ones.

As you set out on your *60 Days to Change*, it's important to know where you stand. You need to know what your financial weaknesses are and which financial habits you need to fix. Financially speaking, no one is perfect. Everyone has *something* to address.

During Week One, your challenge is to identify exactly what *your* weaknesses and bad habits are. These will be a significant part of your focus for the next 60 days. You'll also set your overarching financial goal(s) and establish a series of benchmarks (or "mini-goals") that will help you along the way.

Day 1

Hunt and Gather

Financial struggles, no matter how big or small, generally stem from either a lack of information or a willful blindness to good information that doesn't support your way of thinking. Because information is a prerequisite for smart decision making (financial or otherwise), lacking or ignoring it can lead to the type of bad decisions that characterize the most gruesome financial horror stories.

Take the recent credit crisis. Talk about a bad horror story with a not-so-happy ending. The whole thing had "uninformed bad decision" written all over it.

The abridged version of the story goes something like this: mortgage lenders lent money to uninformed—or at least under-informed—borrowers who couldn't realistically afford to pay it back. These borrowers graciously accepted the lenders' offers and bought houses well outside of their budgets. The housing market tanked. The end.

The sad reality here is that there was plenty of information available to borrowers that would have at least given them pause had they chosen to seek it out. And no doubt many of them received warnings from friends, family and others, yet opted to turn a blind eye to the good advice since it didn't support the goal of being a homeowner.

Decisions made without adequate knowledge are what I like to call "non-decisions." Non-decisions are the gullible, uninformed and laissez-faire choices we make when we rely on the notion that if something *sounds* good or *feels* good it probably *is* good. Or even worse than non-decisions are assertively uninformed bad decisions, i.e., if it sounds too good to be true, count me in!

PETE SAYS:

If you've ever uttered any of the following statements or asked yourself any of these questions after finding yourself in a financial predicament, it's likely that a non-decision landed you there in the first place:

- "Well, how was I supposed to know?"
- "Nobody ever told me that."
- "I didn't know I was doing anything wrong."
- "I had no idea that doing X would lead to Y."
- "Why didn't you tell me that in the first place?"

All of these phrases are rooted in a lack of information, the displacement of blame and an unwillingness to accept responsibility for the consequences of your own actions (or inaction, as the case may be). Don't rely on others to give you the information you need to make important decisions. You have to inform yourself.

The laziness that characterizes non-decisions has the potential not only to lock you into bad arrangements, but also to result in the preservation of a less-than-ideal status quo.

For example:

- You don't know how to refinance your mortgage…
  so you decide not to.
- You don't know how to save money for retirement…
  so you don't.
- You know you could be getting a lower monthly rate on your insurance policy, but you don't know where to begin looking…*so you don't look at all.*

You can avoid these types of non-decisions by equipping yourself with the necessary information *before* making decisions that affect your financial life. Why let non-decisions get in the way of your financial success?

Whether you're rich, poor or somewhere in between, your first task in your *60 Days to Change* is to become financially aware and to quit your non-decision habit cold turkey. The first few days of this program focus on gathering the information you'll need to set your financial goals and benchmarks, so let's get to it!

Below is a checklist of financial information you will need
to gather on Day 1. Go over it and check off the items you
have, or mark the ones that are not applicable.

Yes	No	N/A	**Item**
☐	☐	☐	Bank statements (last 3 months)
☐	☐	☐	Credit card statements (last 3 months)
☐	☐	☐	Student loan details (rate, term, payment)
☐	☐	☐	Car loan details (payment, balance, final payment date)
☐	☐	☐	Pay stubs for all income in the last month
☐	☐	☐	Mortgage details (balance, rate, term, equity, type)
☐	☐	☐	Personal loan details (balance, rate, term, payment)
☐	☐	☐	Auto insurance details (premium, coverage amounts)
☐	☐	☐	Home insurance details (premium, coverage amounts)
☐	☐	☐	Renters insurance details (premium, coverage amounts)
☐	☐	☐	Life insurance details (premium, coverage amounts)
☐	☐	☐	Health insurance details (premium, coverage amounts)
☐	☐	☐	Disability insurance details (premium, coverage amounts)
☐	☐	☐	Any other insurance?
☐	☐	☐	Bank balances (checking and savings)

You're going to be tempted to guess in some places or simply not to look up the accurate details for certain items, but I urge you to take the time to thoroughly gather every item on this list. You will be referring to these items several times over the next 59 days, so getting this out of the way now will make this challenge a lot easier and productive in the long run. If it takes you less than an hour to gather these pieces, consider yourself well organized and off to a great start!

But a word to the wise: being organized isn't by any means the end of the road to financial success, it's merely a skill that will help you get there. Also, just because you're organized in some aspects of your everyday life, don't assume that your good habits will carry over into your financial one.

A stunning example of this comes from a client I worked with a couple of years ago. She was the epitome of well organized and someone I would describe as an "on-top-of-things sort of person." She kept an obsessively clean house, a spotless car and color-coded file drawers that put your accountant (or your financial planner) to shame. Based on her seemingly neurotic compulsion to organize, I assumed she'd be put-together financially speaking as well. I'm sure you can see where this is going. Her financial life was an absolute pigsty. Sure, she'd arranged her bank statements in reverse chronological order, but she clearly hadn't spent even a second looking at any of the statements' details beyond their dates. I took her through every single one of them only to discover two investment accounts that she had forgotten about, a credit card with a small overdue balance (but large, regularly-accruing fees) and a title to her car in her late mother's name.

Long story short, it was at this point that I realized there are some people for whom organization is actually the end objective. For our purposes, however, organization is a tool—a means of keeping on top of your finances in order to move toward your financial goals.

Day 2

Count Your Purchases

Today, you're going to figure out if you suffer from "financial numbness."

What do I mean by that? Think about habits. Habits are funny things. At first we're conscious of them. Then, somehow, good or bad, for better or for worse, they become second nature. Under their spell, we begin to not notice that we're doing them. This can be anything from habits that annoy others (say, cracking our knuckles) to those that eventually harm us. And that's where "financial numbness" and its offshoot, "numb spending," come in.

Numb spending occurs when you're completely oblivious to the number of purchases you make. You practically live in front of the cash register—at the mall, the grocery store, the coffee shop, wherever. The problem is that the more purchases you make, the less discriminating you are in your spending. And it's a slippery slope from this kind of spending to overall financial numbness, which is characterized by a general indifference to the details of your current finances, tackling financial problems or planning for your financial future.

Fiscally smart people take all of their purchases—and their overall financial situation—quite seriously. I'm not suggesting that you get into some sort of Lincoln-Douglas debate with yourself over a pack of gum, but if you're looking to change your financial status you've got to start thinking.

How many times per week, on average, do you make a purchase?

Here's how to find out:

Step 1: Go through your bank and credit card statements and count your purchases for the last month. You gathered these on Day 1, so they should be accessible.

Step 2: Gather all of the cash receipts floating around in your purse or sock drawer. You do save your receipts, right? (The near impossibility of this activity should give you a clear sense of why paying with cash is so tricky—you never really know just how many transactions you've made. But this doesn't mean you get to skip your cash purchases. If you can't find all (or any) of your receipts, take some serious time to think about your cash-spending habits. And if you really don't have any earthly clue as to how many transactions it takes to eat up your cash, it's safe to say that you probably have too many. Controlling the number of purchases you make will be a significant part of your success.)

Step 3: Determine your Monthly Purchase Total by adding the number of credit card and debit card purchases you gathered in Step 1 to the number of cash receipts your unearthed in Step 2. Remember, you're looking for the number of purchases you made, NOT the total value of these purchases. Write that number down.

Step 4: Next, divide your monthly totals by 4.33 to get your Weekly Purchase Total.

What's Your Weekly Purchase Total?

To determine your Weekly Purchase Total, divide your Monthly Purchase Total by 4.33 (the number of weeks in a month).*

Determine Your Monthly Purchase Total:

     Number of monthly credit card purchases   _____

\+   Number of monthly debit card purchases   _____

\+   Number of monthly cash purchases   _____

\=   Monthly Purchase Total   _____

Determine Your Weekly Purchase Total:

_____ / 4.33 = _____

Monthly Purchase Total   Weekly Purchase Total

*Although we're accustomed to thinking of months as having only 4 weeks (28 days), 4.33 is the more accurate number.

> **Step 5:** Compare this number to the Weekly Purchases Scale on the next page. Where do you fall?

Weekly Purchases Scale

Number of Weekly Purchases	Diagnosis
20+ "Pathological Purchaser"	You're out of control. There is simply no reason to spend money three times per day. *Seriously.*
15-19 "Continuously Commercing"	This is darn near unacceptable. If you make this many transactions, chances are you often get to the end of a calendar year and wonder where all of your money went.
10-14 "Moderately Money-Minded"	You seem to have a pretty good grasp of the importance of frugality and economic efficiency, but you have room for improvement.
5-9 "Practically Perfect Purchaser"	This is pretty tough to do, but if you are serious about turning things around, 5-9 weekly transactions is where you want to fall. This probably means: grocery store, gas for you, gas for your spouse, one dinner and two lunches.
1-4 "Seriously Selective Shopper"	You're really broke, really boring or really...financially awesome!

NOTE: If you live in an urban area where you do all your shopping on foot or if you're someone who simply likes to stop off at the store to buy the freshest produce each day, you're probably finding that you easily, and perhaps unfairly, fall into the "Pathological Purchaser" category.

I originally created this chart with the suburban shopper in mind, but I'm also aware that as more and more people try to buy fresh and local, they may not be inclined to do all their grocery shopping in one weekly trip to the supermarket. Daily shopping for fresh produce or for groceries for the day is obviously significantly different from random shopping every day. As a general rule of thumb, if your lifestyle demands you to shop daily for your grocery necessities, automatically subtract five to seven purchases from your total. Be honest with yourself: Only subtract the number of daily grocery trips you make in order to bring your number in line with grocery shopping as a one-time purchase for the week. After all, the point of counting your purchases is to separate regular, necessary purchases from spontaneous, ill-planned ones.

Now that you have your Weekly Purchase Total, you're ready to set your Purchase Goal. Everybody's Purchase Goal is different because everybody has a different disposable income and will be starting from a different point in their financial life. But for the purpose of this book, let's shoot for the stars and assume that you want to make between five and nine transactions per week.

Reducing the number of purchases you make requires forethought and effort. It means taking lunch to work sometimes. It means you can't always go out to dinner on a whim. It means you need to start solving problems with something other than a piece of plastic. If you've determined that you have a purchase "issue" (15 or more purchases per week), you've most likely been meeting everyday needs—eating, transportation, etc.—by making on-the-spot purchases.

Reducing your spending might also require willpower or, in more extreme cases, outside intervention and assistance. For the spender described in the previous paragraph, purchases are a way of solving an immediate need or problem. But there's another kind of Pathological Purchaser. Though I won't go into great detail, this second kind of spender has anything from a habit to a genuine addiction for satisfying themselves with purchases. Whether it's a quick pop into Saks for a new handbag or a cheap pair of earrings at a craft fair (women disproportionately suffer from this problem), this spender buys for reasons that are more complex. If you fall into this latter category of Pathological Purchasers, you may simply need to be more self aware or you may require more serious help to quit a serious addiction. [1]

Before we move on to Day 3, I want to clear up a common misconception. Many of the people who have gone through this program told me that they originally thought that reducing their number of weekly purchases would simply force them to spend more per purchase. It wasn't immediately clear that the Weekly Purchase Total would cut out unnecessary expenditures—these skeptics simply assumed they would learn to buy more during their less-frequent trips to the store. But it won't take you long to realize that the majority of the purchases you're eliminating are those that were completely unnecessary in the first place. Trust me (even you skeptics), you won't need to build more thorough shopping lists; you'll simply cut out superfluous spending.

You're trying to change your life significantly in just 60 days, so you're going to have to commit to making some really tough decisions. You may find you can never do better than "Moderately Money-Minded," but that's okay—at the very least you'll no longer be a victim of numb spending.

---

[1] Source: "Shopping Spree, or Addiction?" www.WebMD.com, 2004

Day 3

Rate Yourself

Everybody gets something different out of their *60 Days to Change*. You'll no doubt find your gains are entirely different from those of your neighbors. That's because everybody has different challenges, all of which will come to light through the course of this challenge. (If your neighbors aren't actually in the program, you should get them involved. Everyone can benefit from a focused 60-day effort to improve their financial life.)

Maybe your goal during these 60 days is to take a chunk out of your debt. Maybe it's time to build an emergency reserve. Or maybe you just need a complete financial lobotomy and brain transplant! The point is, everybody comes into this program because they know they need to achieve something, even if they don't know exactly what that is. That's why on Day 3 you're going to take some time to examine whether you set the proper goals for yourself going into this program.

Answer the following questions as honestly and accurately as possible. Your answers will determine the focus for these 60 days.

DEBT

1. How much credit card debt do you have?
    a. None (0 points)
    b. Less than $3,000 (1 point)
    c. $3,000-$7,000 (2 points)
    d. $7,000-$15,000 (3 point)
    e. More than $15,000 (4 points)

2. How much student loan debt do you have?
    a. None (0 points)
    b. Less than $5,000 (1 point)
    c. $5,000-$10,000 (2 points)
    d. $10,000-$20,000 (3 point)
    e. More than $20,000 (4 points)

3. Do you owe a family or friend any money?
    a. No (0 points)
    b. Yes (3 points)

BUDGETING

1. Do you currently have a monthly budget that you follow?
    a. Yes (0 points)
    b. No (2 points)

2. What is your current monthly surplus of income?
    a. Over $2,000 (0 points)
    b. $1,000-$2,000 (1 point)
    c. $250-$1,000 (2 points)
    d. $0-$250 (3 points)
    e. I have a shortage every month (4 points)

3. How much do you have in your emergency fund?
    a. Six months of expenses (0 points)
    b. Three months of expenses (1 point)
    c. One month of expenses (2 points)
    d. $1,000 (3 points)
    e. Less than $1,000 (4 points)
    f. I don't have an emergency fund (5 points)

RISK MANAGEMENT

1. Are you adequately insured (home, car, life)?
    a. Yes (0 points)
    b. No (3 points)

2. Do you have life insurance outside of your policy at work?
    a. Yes (0 points)
    b. No (2 points)

3. Do you have a will or trust?
    a. Yes (0 points)
    b. No (3 points)

4. Have you formulated a backup plan in case you lose your job?
    a. Yes (0 points)
    b. No (3 points)

> **NOTE:** As you answered these questions, you may have found yourself wondering why you need a life insurance policy outside of the one your job provides you or why, at your age, it makes sense to have a will or a trust. Answers to these questions and others will be provided throughout this book. For now, just keep an open mind about your financial life and avoid accepting that your current financial circumstances are the correct financial circumstances. That just isn't necessarily the case.

There are 11 possible points in each section. Total your points in each section. As you've probably figured out, lower scores are better here (just like in golf). Where did you do best? Where did you do worst?

If you scored **three** points or fewer in any section, you are quite close to mastery in that area of your financial life.

If you scored between **four** and **seven** points in any section, you should expect great results during *60 Days to Change* because this scored indicates targeted focus, which is just what you need to get this ship turned around.

Scoring **eight** points or more, however, indicates that you have let this problem fester for too long. You should be proud of yourself for having started the *60 Days to Change* program because that, my friend, is the first of many small victories that will add up to your ultimate financial success.

Finally, if you scored higher than **eight** in multiple categories, you have a decision to make: Is today going to be the day that you begin turning your financial life around once and for all? Are you going to start with this commitment and continue with an open mind. Well? Are you in?

Your goal will be to improve in each of these areas during your *60 Days to Change*, but you will want to make your weakest area your priority to start.

If you don't think that you struggle with budgeting yet you found yourself with four or more points in one or more categories, you will need to rethink what it really means to manage your budget and to pay special attention during budgeting week (Week Three).

60 Days to Change is designed to help you re-prioritize your finances in the most efficient and cost-sensitive ways possible. So, if after taking this quiz, you feel discouraged thinking about having to pony up more dough for things you didn't even know you needed, *don't*! *60 Days to Change* will help you reorganize and reduce your expenses to afford all the important tools that will make you financially secure. Your goal isn't to spend more money—it's to spend more efficiently.

Day 4

Embrace the Positive

People usually decide to make changes in their lives when they're exposed to pain or stress, and money-induced stress is one of the worst—but most motivating—kinds. You may be reading this book because you're feeling stressed already, but even if you aren't, it's likely that some uncomfortable feelings will surface during these 60 days. All of this will be particularly true if you're sharing your finances with a significant other, as you'll need to deal with their financial stress and stressors in addition to your own. But two of the core goals of this book are to teach you how to deal with these stressors as they arise and to change your money habits in the process.

Because the best way to manage financial stress is to change your thinking, the next challenge will help you learn how to eliminate worry and embrace the positive.

I had a client years ago who loved to focus on what he didn't have. This was not only frustrating to listen to but counterproductive to his work toward his financial goals. He was in a management position at a large manufacturing company, and he constantly complained about the benefits his union employees got and about the overtime bonuses available to them.

He was so worried about what others might be getting that he was not that he failed to notice any advantages he might have. Once I realized this, I encouraged him to take a closer look at his compensation package; in the process we discovered that he had stock options he never knew about. He'd also neglected to see how the workers' overtime hours positively affected his production-based bonuses, meaning that the overtime bonuses he resented actually resulted in a direct increase in his own quarterly bonuses. Just think of the financial gain he could have enjoyed if he had changed his attitude and actually supported his co-workers instead of irrationally competing with them.

And that's exactly what he did. By addressing his stressors and looking for ways to alleviate them, we were able to turn a negative situation into a positive one. But notice that we didn't alter any of the variables here, we simply looked at the situation from a different perspective. A positive one.

In these strange economic times it's easy to focus on the negative. Markets are down, unemployment is up, real estate is a mess and the value of oil is fluctuating like never before. You're constantly inundated by negative news from the TV, radio, Internet, newspapers and so on, but do *you* really have reason to be concerned?

Not necessarily. Obviously, if you've lost your job and your home, you have good reason to be stressed. (Though it is important to remember that no matter how hopeless your financial situation, there is always a solution.) But I've found that many people needlessly panic over their finances. Most of us are on a fixed salary with fixed expenses and needs. Major economic downturns don't have to have a significant impact on our lives. Yes, our investment assets may be affected and we may feel more than ever the importance of saving, but our daily economic realities are largely unchanged. In fact, much of the knee-jerk, reactive panic is self-perpetuating and is itself responsible for some of the downward spiraling of the economy.

So do whatever it takes to change your mind-set from negative to positive, pessimistic to optimistic, panicked to hopeful. You get the picture. I don't mean that you should be delusionally upbeat, but you should aim to focus on the positives rather than to dwell on the negatives, as this will help you feel in charge of—rather than a victim of—your financial life. Allow yourself to be optimistic for a moment by starting off with some sort of positive affirmation: "I have a stable job." "I have great benefits." "I have ten toes." Whatever it takes to turn your gloom into glee. Again, I'm not advocating blind optimism here, rather, that you take the time to consider the positives and use those as a starting place.

Once you've got your rose-tinted glasses on, jot down the three most positive things about your financial life. I've kick-started your list with an entry to get you thinking:

1. I am taking charge of my financial life by going through the *60 Days to Change* challenge, setting my financial goals and working daily to meet them!

2. _____

    _____

    _____

3. _____

    _____

    _____

That wasn't too bad, was it?

Day 5

Get Into a New Financial Mind-Set

Building on the positive outlook you worked on during Day 4, Day 5 takes you a step further to expand that into a complete proactive and optimistic financial mind-set. If you're going to come out of these 60 days with some new positive habits, you need to alter your thinking. Here are seven concepts that will help you get into your new financial mind-set.

1. ***Your life is not about purchases.***
   As Americans we're often planning our next purchase while the ink is still drying on our most recent receipt. And oftentimes we are planning the purchases of things that will ultimately replace the thing we just purchased—like a better car or a bigger house; an in-ground swimming pool instead of the freestanding one that just went up. Americans constantly upgrade perfectly good items, and that's one bad habit you want to unlearn.

2. ***Don't perpetuate the Main Street/Wall Street cliché.***
   Part of the current macroeconomic problems in the U.S. is that both Main Street and Wall Street expect to be bailed out for their failures or missteps. The rhetoric used to explain the causes of this hot mess of a situation does no more than paint an abstract picture

that really just confuses the average person. (And isn't confusion what got us here in the first place?) Seriously, if we can't even keep track of our cash receipts, there's no way we're going to be able to keep up with all of this. As one whose life overlaps with both Wall Street and Main Street, I'm insulted that the economic crisis has been trivialized by simple mind tricks and circular language. In the end, we need to worry less about Wall Street and Main Street as vague metaphors, and instead take personal responsibility for our financial lives and decisions.

3. ***Understand the importance of an emergency fund.***
At the bare minimum, you need about $1,000 to handle most major emergencies. This reserve should not only help you stay out of credit card debt, it should allow you to perform financial triage if an emergency does occur. Your ultimate goal is to secure three months' worth of expenses for your emergency fund, but first things first: find a grand.

4. ***Adopt the phrase "I can't afford it."***
Many a business or life coach will spout the virtues of embracing the phrase "I don't know" when faced with a question you can't answer. When it comes to your financial life, an equally empowering and healthy phrase to adopt is "I can't afford it." And while you're at it, add the phrases "I shouldn't buy it" and "I don't need it" to your personal lexicon.

5. ***If you're within five years of retirement,***
you shouldn't be deep into the market.
This is not an "I told you so" moment, but a concept that now probably seems quite obvious given today's economic realities. If people try to convince you otherwise, just remember that they're likely not going to be willing to supplement your retirement when they're wrong.

6. ***Don't waste your time looking for others to blame.***
Think back to the pull-out box in Day 1. It details the statements
and questions of people who have landed in a predicament thanks
to non-decisions. As illustrated in this box, people are quick to
look outside of themselves when things go wrong and they need
someone to blame. But instead of pointing fingers at others, you
must learn to admit that your financial situation is the result of
your own financial decision making. Maybe someone conned you.
Maybe you made a decision without adequate knowledge. Maybe
someone even stole your identity (although, for your sake, I really
hope not). Hey, maybe you're not even doing so badly. No matter
what landed you in the financial position you are in, you're the only
one who can change it. In short, blaming someone else isn't going
to negate the fact that you—and only you—are responsible for
every ounce of debt you've accrued.

7.

Don't freak out.
You will remember these hard times for the rest of your life,
so make sure you learn from them.

Day 6

Redefine the New Necessities

Chances are you consider many more things "basic life necessities" now than you did 10 or 20 years ago, and that the things you consider to be basic "needs" vary drastically from the things your parents consider basic needs. This is due to what I like to call the "Simplicity-Needs Paradox." The Simplicity-Needs Paradox is the contradiction presented when, in taking steps to simplify your life by decreasing the amount of energy you expend on routine tasks, you increase the number of basic needs necessary to maintain your new level of simplicity.

For example, everyone knows that email is more efficient than snail mail, but in order to have access to email, you have to have a computer. Thus, in order to simplify, you've got to acquire. As we work to simplify your financial life, we're going to have to account for the new necessities that all of us have come to see as basic needs. The question therefore becomes: With so many new necessities, how are we ever going to free up enough money to start saving? But the basic fact of the matter is that we can't start saving until we stop spending. Easier said than done, right?

The following "The New Necessities Exercise" will help you take a bite out of unnecessary spending while still keeping up with the Joneses (or at least with basic culturally current needs). Fill out the questions on the next page, and you'll likely find that you can free up at least $70 per month.

The New Necessities Exercise

Part I
How much do you spend on the following?

New Necessity	Monthly Total
Internet access	_____
Cable/Internet	_____
Coffee addiction	_____
Music	_____
Lunch out	_____
Cell phone	_____

Part II
Where can you cut back?
As you learned on Day 1, organized information can lead to good decision making. Keeping the information from this exercise in mind, you need to carefully analyze your spending on these items to see where you might be able to save.

1. Do you really need the fastest Internet service available? Is there a cheaper plan than the one to which you're currently subscribed? Is there a way to consolidate the services you now get into one lower monthly plan? Assuming I'm not driving you back into the Dark Ages of dial-up, which I wouldn't wish upon anyone, write down the potential monthly savings. $ _____

2.	Do you even watch your premium cable channels? I didn't, so I opted for the lesser package. You might also be able to unsubscribe from certain channels à la carte, which can also reduce your monthly costs. What does the package below yours cost? $_____ How much would you save by unsubscribing from just those premium channels you don't watch or watch infrequently? _____

3.	Do you regularly buy frou-frou coffee drinks? How much would you save if you switched to normal coffee and then doctored it with milk and sugar? $_____

4.	Music can be an addiction, but that doesn't mean you have to buy it. (No, this is not where I'm going to tell you how to how to steal it.) Instead, you can go to most libraries and get CDs to listen to before you buy. This way you can eliminate the cost of the ones you don't like or get your fix and save your dough. Seriously consider this. Even more, consider how much it would save you. $_____

5.	I like overstuffed burritos, too, but there's no reason you can't cut your lunch budget in half. Make a sandwich, keep salad fixings in the fridge at work—just keep the spending at bay. How much money per month can you take off of your lunch spending? $_____

6.	How can you reduce the cost of your cell phone plan? Can you reduce your monthly text message package? Decrease the number of minutes you use each month? Move to the usage plan right below your current one? You'd be surprised by the good customer service at some cell phone service companies—they'll actually act as consultants and sit on the phone with you to help you create a more affordable plan. But you have to be proactive and request help—they usually won't offer this service on their own. How much money can you save with just a couple of small changes? $_____

Determine how much you could save
monthly on The New Necessities

To figure out how much you could be saving each month, add up the monthly totals from the table in Part I. Write that number down. _____
Next, add up the prospective savings you estimated in Part II. Write that number down. _____
Finally, subtract the total you came up with in Part II from the total you came up with in Part I. The resulting number is how much you could be contributing to your emergency fund each month. _____

When I recommend this exercise to clients, I like to tell them about another client of mine, Nadia, who committed to these steps and managed to save $190 per month. She changed her cable plan, reduced the money she spent on lunch during the work week and analyzed her cell phone plan to identify every single area where she could save.

Nadia is a good example of somebody who was wasting a fair amount of money on things she really didn't need (but *thought* she needed).
She didn't cancel her cable; she simply re-evaluated her viewing habits and acted accordingly. She didn't discontinue her cell phone service or even limit her usage; she just discovered that she only used 68% of the minutes she purchased each month and changed plans to take advantage of the savings that come with her level of usage. (The ratio of cell phone usage to rate plan is one that most of us could stand to decrease.) And Nadia's story gets even better: she was ultimately able to put all of her newly "found" money—$2,280 per year to be exact—toward her son's college fund!

Day 7

Park Your Fears

Assuming you're not reading this book because you simply enjoy personal finance books, I'd wager that at some point in the recent past you've acknowledged you could stand to make some changes in your financial lifestyle. This might consist of a few minor adjustments or it could mean a complete financial overhaul, but the fact is that even minor changes can seem daunting. Maybe the sheer prospect of changing anything about your life makes you want to dig in your heels and refuse to alter a single familiar (but bad) habit. The result? You maintain a non-ideal status quo (the devil you know) for fear of facing the unknown (the devil you don't). On Day 7, you're going to come face-to-face with that devil you've for so long been afraid of: change.

Whether you're reading this book knowing you have to change or sensing that change could be good for you, some of the exercises you will undertake and the goals you will set for yourself are going to seem impossible. But keep in mind that just because something seems daunting or impossible at first doesn't mean it is.

What am I talking about? Take, for example, the challenge of reducing your weekly transactions to 10 or fewer. If this seems unreasonable at first, it's likely because you've become accustomed to making frequent purchases to sustain your way of life. I don't want you to feel that positive change results from or depends on sacrifice. Quite the opposite, really. To sacrifice is to give up something you believe you need or deserve. The kind of change we're after results from letting go of things you don't need and letting go of the idea of having the right to things you haven't actually earned.

The fact is change becomes absolutely necessary when your dissatisfaction with the status quo becomes too overwhelming to repress. It's at this point that you have to take a leap of faith, commit to change and assume there's something better out there. I understand this is easier said than done, but initiating change with a positive, empowered attitude is essential to success that lasts. (This doesn't mean you have to be fearless; rather, you are accepting your fears and moving forward without letting them define your every move and decision.)

Now that you've decided that fear is not going to dictate your actions moving forward, let's address them head on. Use the chart on the next page to list your biggest fears about making changes to different aspects of your financial life. What are your worries about managing your debt? About maintaining a budget? About your career and compensation? Once you get these out in the open, your next step is to commit to completing this program: fear will no longer keep you from positive change and the happiness that can result.

FREEDOM FROM FEAR :
The Change Chart

FACTORS OF FINANCIAL FREEDOM	MY FEARS AND CONCERNS
A positive mind-set	
Debt management	
Controlling my spending	
Maintaining my budget	
My ability to identify and mitigate risk	
My career and compensation	
Developing a savings plan	
Evaluating major purchases	
A permanent plan for success	

Now, I want you to commit yourself, right now, to looking past those fears and continuing through this program.

The 60 Days to Change Pledge

I, _____, promise to do it—to take a hard, honest look at my financial life and keep going with my *60 Days to Change* I may be scared, but, for reasons that matter, I've got to do it.

I owe it to myself, to my family and friends, and to my future.

I can do it. I am capable of amazing things. Starting today, tackling the seemingly impossible is my top priority.

_____

Signature   Date

Week Two

Deal With Credit, Debt and Other Skeletons in Your Financial Closet

Where there's credit, there's often debt. You could say that the two are connected at the hip, but that doesn't mean their relationship is always a healthy one. If you ask me, credit and debt are a bit needy, a little too codependent for my taste. That's not to say these two are always going to spell financial trouble, but when it comes to getting your financial life in order, there's no way to avoid at least a cursory discussion of what roles, if any, they play.

It will become increasingly apparent as we trek through these 60 days that there are several components that shape your financial health. Credit and debt are only two of them, but they have the potential to play a very large role. That's because easy, ready credit has introduced debt to the general consumer on a mass scale.

Not too long ago, borrowing money was a much more formal process. People had to go to their financial institutions and prove themselves worthy of borrowing and paying back money in a timely manner. And most people only did this when making a significant purchase—a car, a home, a business, college tuition, etc.—or if they were facing an unforeseen expense such as a new roof or a large medical bill. But this has all changed. At some point during the last few decades, other institutions began realizing there was money to be made by offering consumers the ability to buy their goods and services with ease. There was also money to be made from interest on these loans. Large department stores began extending credit to customers as a way of getting them to buy what they wanted, when they wanted it. You've probably noticed that the concept of putting an item on layaway until you can afford it is almost (though not entirely) extinct these days. Stores have made it so that you can buy it now—independent of whether or not you can afford it.

If you're a college student (or were a college student in the last 15 years), you're likely all too familiar with the booths that credit card companies set up on campus to sign you up for credit lines. They offer free T-shirts and other promotional items in hopes of enticing you to register for their card on your way from Biology 101 to English Lit. Your mailbox is no doubt brimming over with offers to consolidate your credit cards into one easy payment with a competing credit card company at 0% interest for the first year.

Everyone's in on the act. Airlines offer free miles with the use of their credit cards. Department stores will give you 10% off your first purchase if you sign up for theirs. And even gas station chains have jumped on the private-credit card bandwagon, luring you in with offers of free gas for every dollar you put on their handy cards.

Why?

Because credit leads to debt, debt leads to interest and interest leads to profit for the issuing companies. Some of these companies actually make more money on interest from their credit cards than on the services or products they provide. Why do you think that car dealer was so anxious to give you a loan when you bought your last car?

Assuming you're one of the millions of American who has a love-hate relationship with credit, in Week Two you'll learn everything you need to know to rid your closet of financial skeletons. Though you might not be out of debt at the end of your 60 days, you'll certainly be armed with a plan and some tools that will help you get there sooner than you ever thought possible. Our goal this week is to raise your credit and debt awareness, no matter what your current level of consciousness may be. This may sting a bit, but trust me: you'll come out stronger because of it.

Day 8

Order Your Credit Report

My clients often ask me what I define as a "spending problem." My general answer is that if you're spending more money than you make, you've got a spending problem. With the increased availability and ease of obtaining credit over the last couple of decades, it's not very often that you meet someone who doesn't have at least some type of debt. So does this mean that everybody has a spending problem? Not exactly.

Degrees of debt vary and not all debt is created equal. For the most part, we think of debt as a negative thing—and for the most part, it is—but there is such a thing as "good debt." This is the kind of debt that builds your credit and in the process raises your credit score. Many debt experts will tell you that debt is an intelligent use of leverage, which is true. Yet most people are in debt because they've bought things they couldn't afford, not because they were being strategic spenders. I would like to tell you that the solution to debt is simply to stop buying things you can't afford, but it's a bit more complicated than that. Why? Sometimes people buy things they can't afford because they're not aware they can't afford them.

Huh?

Many people associate available credit with purchasing power. They rationalize, "If a credit institution is willing to issue me credit, they must have confidence that I'll be able to pay it off." But a credit institution has just a little conflict of interest when it comes to determining what you can and cannot afford, wouldn't you say? Just think about all those people whose creditors gave them a vote of confidence to buy houses they couldn't afford if you need an example.

So what's the point of having good credit if you can't afford to use it to buy the things you want?

That's the great financial paradox. You want to obtain and build credit so that you qualify to receive the best terms possible from creditors. (After all, without good credit how are you going to be able to afford those things that you can't pay for completely, up front, in cash, but that you actually really can afford?) On the flip side, if you *do* qualify for good credit terms, it's likely because you're the type of person who would never think of using credit to buy things you can't realistically afford (or aren't able to pay off within a reasonable amount of time).

But the point of getting and improving your credit is not so that you can *buy more things.* Good credit is important because:

- **Healthy credit indicates healthy habits.** As far as many decision makers are concerned, discipline and structure in one aspect of your life tend to be a good indication of a consistent pattern of responsible habits. Your credit is one of the easiest entry points of assessment, which is why you need to determine your credit health today.

- **Some employers are now running credit checks.** Can you imagine being the best candidate for a job, but losing out on it because you have bad credit? Federal law prevents employers from discriminating based on bankruptcy, but employers are allowed to base their hiring decisions on collection actions and defaults.

- **You need at least decent credit to set up basic household utilities, such as electricity, water and phone service.** A seemingly harmless series of impulsive credit card purchases that wind up doing near-fatal damage to your credit score can create a nightmare when you try to set up accounts with utility companies. What's it going to be? Stuff? Or electricity, gas and running water? (This is not a trick question. The answer is electricity, gas and running water.)

- **In many instances, poor credit will prevent you from renting an apartment or house.** Being denied a mortgage is one thing; being denied a place to rent, though? That puts you in a completely different category. It means you'll be stuck at home with Mom and Dad, or worse, turning a friend into a roommate. You can imagine what this type of situation does for relationships. Yikes.

- **Many insurance companies will charge you a higher monthly premium if you have suspect credit.** Yep, it's the equivalent of a health insurance company charging higher premiums for those with high cholesterol, high blood pressure and obesity. The company essentially sees a higher risk and sets fees accordingly.

The good news is, with *60 Days to Change,* you're working to improve your credit, which will give you the power to change all of these.

Bad Credit vs. Good Credit

People with bad credit want to improve their credit so they can purchase things they can't afford. But people with bad credit have a hard time improving their credit because they've already purchased things they can't afford. (That's why they have bad credit.)

vs.

People with good credit are those who purchased things they *could* afford and *did* pay off. But people with good credit generally don't buy things they can't realistically afford to pay off in a reasonable amount of time. (That's why they have good credit.)

Your credit standing is an indication of your financial health and your relationship with debt, not a permission slip to buy more *stuff*. Consider your credit report a type of "debt report card." The better your credit history, the better your relationship with debt and vice versa.

How do I find out where I stand with creditors?

On Day 8, you're going to order a copy of your credit report. If you have good credit, your credit report will simply reinforce the importance of your good financial habits. If you have bad credit, your credit report will confirm your need to develop new financial habits and get rid of old ones. If you have no idea what to expect either way, well, there's even more incentive for you to order a copy today.

You can order your credit report online at www.AnnualCreditReport.com. If you don't have access to the Internet, you can call 1-877-322-8228.

> **NOTE:** You might be wondering why I chose AnnualCreditReport.com over the other credit reporting services out there. You might also be wondering why some services are free while others charge you fees.
>
> The basic credit report obtained from AnnualCreditReport.com won't give you your credit score, but it will give you your credit history. You only need basic information about your credit during your 60 Days to Change, and I find that people who manage their credit health by aiming to reach an arbitrarily-selected credit score aren't as successful as those who manage their credit by continually improving their financial habits. (I discuss this in more detail on Day 9.)

Basic Reports vs. Enhanced Reports

As I mentioned above, for the purposes of this book, you'll just need to order a basic report. (I detail the elements of a basic credit report later in this chapter.) In the process you're likely to come across the option to purchase an enhanced report—something that might interest you in the future, but which there's no need for now. While an enhanced report will include features such as score tracking, fraud alerts and credit monitoring, it comes with a price tag. Although those features might eventually be helpful to you, they aren't necessary at this point since we're focusing on managing your habits rather than your credit score.

The Free-Credit-Report Saga

One saying in the financial world—or the business world in general—is "There's no such thing as a free lunch." Nowhere is this more true than in the credit reporting industry, where deceptive practices run rampant. Consumer deceit is so prevalent that the Federal Trade Commission (FTC) recently sued multiple imposter credit reporting websites that claimed to be free when, in actuality, they weren't free at all.[1]

---

[1] Source: http://www.ftc.gov

Case in point? The very popular FreeCreditReport.com has been the target of much consumer anger and confusion (as well as FTC scrutiny). The website offers its members free credit reports, but to be a member, you have to pay a monthly fee. It seems simple enough, right? But with that same logic, a television is free as long as you buy the box it comes in. And the box costs the price of a television.

I purchased access to TrueCredit.com when I began my research for this book and was quite impressed with their services. But I ultimately found that their services don't emphasize the importance of developing good spending habits; they focus, instead, on improving your credit score. Your focus on the path to becoming financially solid should be to develop sound critical-thinking skills in regard to your money and how you spend it.

One of the real negatives of obtaining your credit report from any of these online services is that they all relentlessly try to sell you something. While researching this book, I purchased multiple credit reports from different agencies. I was asked to buy enhanced services multiple times on top of the enhanced services I had already purchased. How enhanced can one report get? Too enhanced for me, apparently.

What to Look for on Your Credit Report

Now that I have my credit report, what am I supposed to do with it?

For now, you want to familiarize yourself with the rich information it provides you. Instead of just looking at your credit score, look at the following items to see where you stand:

_____ **Total Accounts**
This is the total number of accounts listed on your credit history. As with most items on your credit report, this number can vary with each credit reporting agency.

_____ **Open Accounts**

This is the total number of accounts you currently have open—whether they have balances or not. A zero-balance account is still considered open.

_____ **Closed Accounts**

This lists all closed credit lines. This could include old mortgages, closed credit cards or paid-off student loans.

_____ **Delinquent**

This section details any accounts for which you are behind on payments. Inevitably, this is the section that surprises most people. It is not uncommon to find delinquent accounts that you didn't know about.

_____ **Derogatory**

Whereas a 30-day late payment is considered delinquent, a 60-day late payment is considered derogatory. This section is the most important, as anything really hurting your credit will show up here.

_____ **Balances**

What do you owe the world? More specifically, what do you owe your creditors? That number will show up in this section, and it can be pretty scary if you've taken out expensive loans for things such as a mortgage or college tuition.

_____ **Payments**

This is the section that lists your monthly debt obligations. This will include your monthly mortgage and/or car payments, minimum payments on your credit card(s) and other loans.

_____ **Public Records**

This section lets you know that if your credit problems have become public record. It includes liens, foreclosures, bankruptcies and legal judgments. This section will also list any changes in your marital status and whether you have sought professional credit counseling.

—— **Inquiries** (2 years)
This section indicates which people or institutions have requested your credit report in the last two years. These inquiries are usually the result of your requests or applications to borrow money from an institution. This is called a "hard inquiry." A hard inquiry is an inquiry initiated by someone on the verge of lending you money per your request, whereas a "soft inquiry" is initiated by someone checking your credit to see if you are a good credit risk. A soft inquiry is usually performed by an insurance company or an employer. Too many hard inquiries are a bad thing and will harm your credit.

Full Disclosure: I went seven years without checking my credit report. It wasn't because I didn't think it was important, it was because I didn't think I had a reason to check it. I paid my bills on time, I didn't miss payments and I made enough money to cover my purchases. When I finally took the time to check my credit, however, I was shocked to find that I had an account in collection. Considering my spending habits, I was furious that my credit report didn't reflect my stellar (if I do say so myself) spending habits, but the explanation for my problem was quite simple: I never closed an old checking account. In my mind, I was done using it, but instead of closing it I let it sit unused for four years. There was $50 in the account when I stopped using it and, over the years, I started acquiring inactivity fees—$3 per month, to be exact. The account fell below zero and the bank was unable to contact me at my old business address. That's when the account went into collection, sending "Perfect Credit Pete" to the dark side. I was able to make the proper arrangements to pay the fee and get my credit headed back in the right direction. The lesson? Register for a free credit report every year, take the time to review it and follow up on any negative findings. (We'll discuss *how* on Day 9.) Otherwise, you could be in for some nasty credit surprises in the future.

Day 9

Repair and Build Your Credit

As you may have gathered on Day 8, I'm a big advocate of improving spending habits rather than focusing on credit scores. But because improving your habits will improve your credit score and because this number will play an important role once your financial life is back in order, it's important that you understand how these two things are related.

What Your Credit Score Means

Assigning a numeric value to your credit profile is a structured way for creditors (as well as employers and utility and insurance companies) to gauge your credit standing relative to others.

Your credit score will range somewhere between 300 and 850. As a point of reference, a score of 700 puts you in a better position than 61% of the nation. And a score of 765 puts you ahead of 84% of your fellow Americans. One of the most common questions people ask me is, "What qualifies as a good credit score?" While I often hesitate to answer the question (because I find it to be irrelevant), the answer is 725. A score of 725 is technically good. But anything above 700 should allow you receive the credit lending terms that you desire.

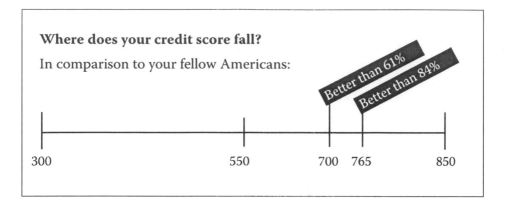

Where does your credit score fall?

In comparison to your fellow Americans:

Better than 61%

Better than 84%

300 550 700 765 850

Don't get me wrong: having a point of reference against which to gauge your relative standing is definitely a positive thing, but as humans we always manage to make things more confusing than they need be. Take, for example, my personal credit score. It has a 69-point spread, which means that among the three major credit reporting agencies, one of them rates me 69 points higher than the lowest agency's scoring model. What am I to gather from this? That's easy: I shouldn't manage the score; I should manage my habits. If you manage your habits, your credit score will take care of itself, and eventually you can use it as a tool to track your progress.

Yesterday, you ordered your credit report and noted your standing in a number of areas. And today, we're going to start down the arduous path to fixing your credit—that is, assuming it's "broken." ("Broken" is my highly technical term for a credit report that contains *any* negative elements which affect your credit.) Your credit as a whole may or may not be broken, but we want to address *anything* that needs improvement. Of course, when it comes to fixing broken credit, there's a catch: you can't technically fix it.

Why not?

Your past indiscretions can't be fully erased. Your financial history will always be a part of your credit record. The good news is that you *can* significantly improve your credit, and with a little time and effort it *will* get better.

What Credit Scores and Dieting Have in Common

Many people assess their credit health based on their ability to meet a credit score that falls into some lender's definition of "good credit." My suggestion is to think about your credit score as weight on a scale. The number you see there is not in and of itself a measure of whether you're overweight or too thin—to determine that, you would need to know other details like height, muscle mass and the like—but it does have value as an indication of your relative progress (or setback) over time.

Think about it. Many variables factor into a person's weight, so when creating dieting benchmarks, one has to take into consideration factors like bone structure, age, muscular composition and so on, rather than to try to meet a goal set forth by a universal weight chart that maps out pounds versus height. Everyone will have different diet goals based on their own unique combination of contributing variables.

So, just as you wouldn't base your diet success on meeting a weight that doesn't take your body type into consideration, you shouldn't base your credit health on a score that doesn't factor in your starting point, the steps you've taking to improve it and the healthy spending habits you've developed as a result. That's a surefire recipe for disappointment. Instead, you should view a rise or fall in your credit score as a means of calibrating your habits in order to offset setbacks or perpetuate progress.

How do I get started?

7 Steps to Improving Bad Credit
(Or to maintaining good credit)

1. **Look for any disputable items on your credit report.**
   Because I'm a perennial optimist, I tend to think that if there's a blemish on my credit report, it can't possibly be my fault. Of course, this might be more delusional than optimistic, but you should start your credit repair process by going through your credit report closely to make sure that there are no inaccuracies such as a misspelled name, credit lines that you never applied for or obvious cases of identity theft.

2. **Dispute any inaccuracies.**
   There are several ways to dispute inaccuracies on your credit report that don't require working with a credit repair service. These services don't do anything you can't do on your own. But if you don't want to go through the process of disputing these items, you can certainly hire a professional to help.

Assuming you decide to go it alone, begin by filling out the online form at one of the credit bureaus' websites or by calling their toll-free phone numbers.

The U.S. has three major credit reporting agencies. You will need to get in touch with at least one, but it's wise to file a dispute with all three. These phone numbers change frequently, but those listed below are current as of this writing.

Experian	**TransUnion**	**Equifax**
p: 1-888-397-3742	p: 1-800-916-8800	p: 1-800-685-1111
w: Experian.com	w: Transunion.com	w: Equifax.com

Identifying inaccuracies in your credit report

As you go through your credit report, keep in mind that many of the items you might think are disputable actually aren't. For instance, people often want to dispute the timing of a payment but lack the documentation to support the dispute. There isn't a single person with bad credit who doesn't believe he or she paid a bill within the given grace period. Can you imagine if credit agencies addressed this type of dispute?

The table below will give you a good idea of what you should contest and what you shouldn't even bother with:

Disputable	Non-disputable*
The timing of payments (with documentation)	The timing of payments (without documentation)
Fraud	The level of interest you are being charged
Outdated information	
	Your own poor decision-making
Clerical errors such as a wrong name, address or account number	
	Whether a bankruptcy is your fault or not

*If what you've identified as an inaccuracy is not disputable, you're going to have to improve your credit report the old-fashioned way. See steps 3 through 7 to learn how.

3. **Only carry and use one credit card.**
   There's no reason to have more than one active credit card.
   That means no store credit cards—even if you have to forfeit the
   enticing discount you would receive upon opening a new account.
   You damage your credit when you open a line of credit and then
   cancel it. If you currently have a store card, don't cancel it. Just get it
   to a zero balance, make sure there are no annual fees and cut it up.

4. **Maintain an "availability-to-utilization ratio" of 2:1.**
   In other words, don't max out your cards. Your credit will take a
   serious beating if you reach your available balance. Your balance
   should not exceed higher than 50% of your available credit. Your
   score can start getting dinged at as low as 35%, but anything above
   50% will leave you hurting.

5. **Don't cancel a credit card with a long credit history.**
   Once you cancel the card, the evidence that you have a good credit
   history also disappears.

6. **Pay your bills on time.**
   A person with a modest credit score can improve his or her score as
   much as 20 points by simply paying bills on time for one month. If this
   is an area where you could stand to improve, make it your goal to make
   at least the minimum payment on each of your bills this month. From
   there, try to do the same each month after that.

7. **Use credit but wisely.**
   Just make sure to take it easy. Charge a nominal amount each month
   and pay it off. If you charge $75 per month and promptly pay it off,
   you'll be on your way to building some very solid credit.

NOTE: By choosing to use credit on only one expense each month—be it groceries or gas—you are not only working towards building a healthy credit history but also towards sharpening your discipline.

When it comes to spending on credit, discipline goes hand in hand with simplicity. Say you've selected groceries (or another recurring, regular expense) as the monthly expense you're going to put on your credit card and pay off each month. But somewhere along the way you forget and use your credit card for car fuel and maintenance. Whether you know it or not, you have just made a giant mistake. The point of selecting one category is to develop discipline by exercising simplicity. The more spending categories you add to this exercise, the more likely you are to develop poor spending habits. Soon enough, you'll be using your credit card for various other expenditures, which will put you at higher risk of accumulating debt and send you back to square one.

I emphasize discipline because there really are no shortcuts in this process. You must pay your bills on time, use one credit card, put minimal charges on your credit card each month and pay it off when you do. These are the types of habits that will help you improve your credit and, yes, eventually, even your credit score.

Day 10

Create a Debt Pay-Down Plan

At risk of stating the obvious, I always tell my clients that if they don't set their goals, they'll never achieve them.

In Week One, we set your goal for the entire 60-day program. Today, we're going to focus on your debt, set realistic goals for paying it off and create an actionable plan to do so. Your debt pay-down plan will become particularly powerful when combined with the budget you'll create next week, but let's not get too far ahead of ourselves. For now, let's talk debt.

Every bad habit comes equipped with a healthy dose of denial. Debt is no different. Over the years, I've compiled a mental archive of the different ways people try to either rationalize their debt away or blame it on someone else. Here are some of my favorites:

> "My finances were in good shape until I got those unexpected medical bills in the mail."

> "I had to take out a ton of student loans because my parents neglected to save for my college education."

"The TV was on sale. I would have been dumb not to buy it at that price."

"My car was out of warranty, and I hate driving a car that isn't under warranty."

"I was throwing money away by renting, so it only made sense to buy."

"Our family hadn't been on a vacation in three years. We couldn't afford it, but hey, I didn't want to look like a cheapskate."

The list goes on. But no matter how good your excuse is, there's no gray area when it comes to debt—you're either in it or you're not. And if you're in it, it can only be tackled through discipline, patience and proper planning. As you begin to think about your debt, remember one thing: a debt is a debt is a debt. Don't ignore the "12 months same as cash" debt you accrued when you bought your new couch on the promise of no interest for a year. Don't ignore your student loans, even if they're in deferment. (While deferment does allow you to delay your payments, doing so simply puts off the inevitable.) If you owe money to any company, person or other entity, it counts toward your debt total. Compartmentalizing your debt into arbitrary categories merely detracts from your progress.

While we're only dedicating one day to the creation of your debt pay-down plan, it could take months or even years for you to get yourself completely out of debt, depending on the amount of debt you have. Don't be discouraged by the impending hard work, though; this plan will get you on a regular payment schedule, help you stay organized and make your financial stress progressively easier to manage.

Create Your Debt Pay-Down Plan

Step 1: Map out your debt.

Before you figure out how you're going to pay off your debt, you need to figure out what debt you actually have. To do this, list all of your debts, from smallest to largest, in the table. Allow yourself as much time as necessary to complete this table—and make sure not to leave out any details.

Whom do you owe?	Amount owed	Interest rate	Minimum payment	Are your payments current?

Step 2: Build momentum with small debt victories.

Don't make equal payments on each debt; it's inefficient. Start by focusing on paying off your smallest debt and getting the balance down to zero. This will free up the money you were putting toward the monthly minimum payment so you can put it toward the next debt, not to mention that it will help you create a sense of financial momentum.

> **NOTE:** If you're wondering why we're focusing on the lowest balance instead of the highest interest rate, it's because we're trying to create momentum and zero balances. So, at this point, try not to concern yourself with the interest rates (even though I know it goes against conventional wisdom).
>
> Creating small victories and zero balances up front is the financial equivalent of losing that first five pounds on a diet. You just need some confirmation that what you're doing really works! As you pay off these balances, you'll begin to accumulate the money you were once putting toward minimum payments each month, allowing you to apply those savings to the next-lowest balance on your list.

Step 3: Commit to a debt-payment schedule.

This process is as simple as it gets, assuming you commit to making it part of your routine. The key is to just keep chipping away at the debt. Sure, it will take time, but it will also work. Every time you free up money in your budget using a tip from *60 Days to Change*, apply it to your next-lowest balance.

As a personal finance expert, I'm always tempted to create complicated processes for debt liquidation. But the reality is you need a very simple plan that's easy to stick to. Debt liquidation is way too important to complicate with confusing financial algorithms and impossible goals.

Financial Momentum

Financial momentum is one of the master themes of this book. Almost every one of the exercises here will allow you to get your financial train moving. Have you ever tried to pull a car? Neither have I, but I hear that once the car starts rolling it's easier to pull. And that's because the initial motion creates momentum, making the task a lot more feasible.

You'll discover that by completing each exercise in this book, you're simultaneously making the next one easier. That's because you're picking up financial momentum each day.

Day 11

Debt Reality Check

Debt doesn't discriminate. It can sneak up on you when you're least expecting it. So if you're in debt, don't for a minute think that it's because you're a failure or subject to some divine retribution or that you're at the receiving end of some bad karma. As it turns out, debt is more a matter of physics than karma. The reason you're in debt is because when life presented you with a certain set of circumstances, you responded by spending money you didn't have. Good or bad, right or wrong, that's how it happened. And that's all there is to it.

So whether you consider yourself a good person or a bad person, a victim of karma or of physics, there are certain debt realities you need to accept. Some of these are new, some you've already heard, but on Day 11, you're going to commit them to memory once and for all. And, yes, there will be a quiz at the end of this chapter, so study hard!

1. **The best way to start climbing out of a hole is to stop digging it.**
   If you're committed to getting out of debt, you're going to have to stop spending money irresponsibly. That makes enough sense, right? Right,

but it wasn't exactly your propensity for rational thinking or logical reasoning that got you into this situation, so it's likely not going to get you out either. (Although I'd like to think there's a chance it might). Often, irrationality takes over at the time of purchase. Have you ever incurred debt to buy something that you thought would impress your friends? To buy a gift for someone else? Or even to buy something you really wanted but didn't necessarily need? I could go on. The point is that there are many other purchasing circumstances just like these, but none of them is rational and none of them justifies going into debt.

2. **There's no reason to have more than one major credit card (Visa, MasterCard, Discover or American Express).**
Getting down to just one card should be one of your primary goals. Many people have multiple credit cards because they couldn't get a high enough credit limit with just one card. That's a big no-no. Just because an institution offers you credit doesn't mean you should take it or that you can afford to take on that much debt. Keep the card with the longest credit history. Cancel and get rid of any other cards.

3. **Don't open any store credit cards. It just doesn't make sense.**
Your one major credit card will buy the same things that the store card will. Yes, you might save 10 or 15 percent on your purchase, but it's not worth the credit risk. Every new credit line you open increases your chances of overextending yourself.

4. **You can't have everything you want or even everything you think you need.**
Did you find a great pair of shoes to match that purse you haven't carried in years? Maybe, but that doesn't mean that you have some sort of cosmic approval to ignore your debt situation and purchase them. If I can make another dieting reference, think about what Oprah said about food: "Nothing tastes as good as *thin* feels." By the same token, no purchase makes you feel as good as being debt free does.

5. **Buying something on a "12 months same as cash" or "no interest for a year" basis is never a good idea.**
   Pay for it now or don't buy it at all. Life can change, and you may be in a worse financial situation 12 months from now. In the 12 months between the time that you "purchase" the item and when you actually pay for it, numerous financial challenges could arise. You could lose your job, incur emergency expenses of another nature or even incur more debt. Why risk this? If you can think of a scenario in which it makes sense, you are wrong. Twice.

6. **Your student loans shouldn't be an afterthought.**
   In fact, they may require the most thought. After all, what other debt can you accumulate so freely when you don't have an income to justify it? Yes, you're allowed to defer student loans. You're also allowed to spend hours at an all-you-can-eat buffet. But neither is a particularly good idea.

   I realize that this might be antithetical to other advice you might have received about student loans. Many people have been told they should just keep paying the minimum on their student loans since the interest rate and monthly payment are both lower than those of their credit cards. Also, because I often recommend paying off your lowest debt, you might think school loans are a logical option to push aside since there is a good chance they don't meet this criterion. But school loans are a little bit different (and more confusing) than most of your other loans in that they can't be classified as a depreciating or an appreciating asset.

   For instance, your home is (generally) an appreciating asset. That means that it will increase in value over time. Many people aren't in a hurry to pay off a 30-year mortgage because during the pay-down the home is actually increasing in value. Your car is a depreciating asset, meaning that by the time you pay it off, it's often worth less than what you paid for it. The old rule of thumb is to pay off all depreciating assets before appreciating assets. And while your education is an asset, it's neither appreciating nor depreciating. Student loans are simply debt—debt that you must get rid of as soon as possible. The sooner you pay this debt off, the sooner it will stop stifling your financial life. It's like the old marathoner's creed: the faster you run, the sooner you're done.

Bottom line: don't avoid the inevitable. Start paying the loans back as soon as possible.

7. **Don't get caught up in the transfer game.**
    Constantly transferring credit card balances to cards with lower interest rates is a losing proposition. *60 Days to Change* is a program designed to help you face your financial life head on. While transferring your credit card debt to a card with a lower interest rate can seem like a good thing, more often it is a waste of time, energy and focus. In extreme cases it can be prudent, but, in general, obtaining a lower rate on your credit card simply treats the symptoms and not the problems.

    I have seen it for years: people in debt often get in a game of opening new lines of credit with lower interest rates in order to address their growing debt problem. What people tend to ignore are the 3% to 8% transfer fees often associated with transferring card balances. This means that a $10,000 balance transfer could cost you as much as $800. You need to pay off your debt in a systematic, structured way. Playing the transfer game only dilutes focus and incurs new fees.

If you understand these debt realities, you'll be well on your way to breaking the debt cycle. At the very least, lack of knowledge will no longer be an excuse.

Pop Quiz:
Do you need a debt reality check?

Yes   No   *Answer the questions below to see where you stand.*

☐   ☐   Are you currently carrying a balance on your credit card that won't get paid off at month's end?

☐   ☐   Do you have more than one major credit card?

☐   ☐   Do you have store credit cards? Credit cards with perks like frequent-flyer miles? Gas-station credit cards? In other words, do you have any credit cards other than your one major credit card?

☐   ☐   Do you buy what you want, regardless of your financial standing?

☐   ☐   Are you currently paying for an item with "12 months same as cash" credit?

☐   ☐   Do you have any student loans in deferment?

☐   ☐   Does your emergency plan consist of using credit?

☐   ☐   Have you opened up a credit card solely to save money on a particular purchase in the last 12 months?

☐   ☐   Does it take you longer than two seconds to calculate the number of credit cards you have?

☐   ☐   Have you ever transferred a credit card balance in order to get a lower interest rate?

☐   ☐   Have you received a "collection call" in the past 12 months?

☐   ☐   Are you currently paying only the minimum payments on all of your lines of credit?

☐   ☐   Do you currently fund holiday purchases with credit?

If you answered "yes" to any of these questions, then it's time to get real with yourself. Your debt pay-down plan will only work if you introduce some behavioral changes into your financial regimen. If you're accruing debt as fast as you're paying it off, you'll be catching up, not paying down. Keep this in mind: if you don't change your habits on your own, a negative external factor will do it for you.

Day 12

Personal Loans from Family and Friends

If you're in debt, there's a reasonable chance you owe money to a family member or friend. This type of debt doesn't affect your credit score, but it certainly doesn't help you become a financially responsible human being.

People who take loans from friends and family usually do so with good intentions. They tell themselves that they "just need a little help from a loved one," but these types of loans can be the riskiest ones of all. It comes down to this: banks are in the business of lending money, so if you can't get a loan from a bank it's likely because they believe your risk of default is quite high. When bank lenders evaluate your loan application, they base their decision to give you a loan or not on your ability to pay them back on schedule (loan schedules tend to be fairly reasonable—that is, if you can afford them). If they reject you, it's likely because they don't believe you can live up to reasonable terms. And if the experts can't justify giving you money, it's safe to say that you're putting your friends and family in a precarious situation by asking them to do the same. Why place this burden (and risk) on people you love?

In tenuous financial times, family or friend loans can become a great source of tension between lender and borrower. That is, a great source of tension between your parents, your best friend or your cousin...and YOU.

In order to understand this problem, let's look at the situation from the lender's perspective.

> *It looks like Tim needs some money. I would do anything to help him, but he does make some really strange money decisions. He drives a really nice car, he wears expensive clothes and he always eats out. I can't believe he doesn't have any money to pay his bills. Wait a second! Of course he doesn't have any money—he spent it all on his car, clothes and lunches. But what kind of parent would I be if he had to struggle financially because I said no to him? I think I can afford to help him, but I don't really know. My expenses are increasing as I get older. Then again, if I can get him out of this bind, I'll feel better and I won't feel the terrible guilt of not helping my son.*

Not only is this situation awkward for your family, but it also distances you from them. Is a lifestyle you can't afford really more valuable than the most important relationships in your life? Why waste your time, money and effort trying to be something you're not? Why pretend you can afford things you can't, when in the end you're going to end up creating a negative reality that will far outweigh the positive illusion you were aiming for with all that overspending?

It's incredibly difficult to find yourself on either side of this equation. Saying "no" to a family member isn't easy, but it's often the right thing for everyone.

"The best way to learn how to thrive financially is to struggle financially. Financial challenges are in our lives to help us develop our financial skills."

Some people might consider this advice callous, but it's really not. Callous is perpetuating someone's delusions of grandeur and their unrealistic debt load.

You might be thinking that this just really isn't the case with the people who loaned you money. In fact, they seemed quite happy to do it. But trust me, this is a common mind-set. And I can tell you now that it's the result of one of two typical scenarios, each of which makes asking your loved ones for money seem harmless and sometimes (gasp) even pleasurable:

1. The person you're borrowing from, for some reason, seems to think it is a good idea.

2. The person you're borrowing from either calls it a gift or alludes to the fact that you may not have to pay them back.

Sure, these are enticing traps, but the bottom line is it's time to take off the training wheels. You simply can't be a self-sustaining, fully-functioning person if you have to borrow money from your friends and family.

Commit to it. Say it out loud: "BORROWING FROM MY FAMILY AND FRIENDS IS NOT AN OPTION."

If you currently have an outstanding debt to a family member or friend, you must make an effort to start paying it back during your 60 Days to Change. On Day 12, you're going to start by making amends to the person (or people) you owe. On the next page you'll find the "*60 Days to Change* Payback Commitment" form. Copy it, fill it out and give it to the person who loaned you money.

60 Days to Change Payback Commitment

I, _____, have borrowed money from you. I really appreciate the trust you placed in me when you loaned me this money. I also realize that I haven't done the best job of paying you back in a timely fashion. This may or may not be a big deal to you, but I have just made it a big deal to me.

I owe you $_____. I borrowed this money from you when I had a financial problem. My financial problem then became your financial problem. I am in the process of rectifying this.

Please understand that while I have made my debt to you a major priority, I still have other financial obligations. I will start paying you back systematically, starting immediately. I will pay you a sum of $_____ every month. I will also increase this payment when possible.

Thank you again for believing in me and my ability to pay you back. Our relationship means too much to me to take this borrowed money for granted.

_____

Signature   Date

Day 13

Explore a Refinance

Owning a home is an important and often involved financial process. What do I mean by "process"? If you're asking this question, it's likely you've never owned a home.

A mortgage is one instrument that transforms home ownership from an ordinary purchase into a process. Ironically, many of the same people who struggle to commit to a New Year's resolution have no problem signing their names to this 30-year contract. Sometimes people even sign terrible mortgage contracts (see "Four Types of Mortgages to Avoid" below) just to "get into" the home they want.

What do I mean by "get into"? There are two answers. The obvious one is that people often commit to terrible mortgages to buy houses they really can't afford. As a result they get stuck with high interest rates and virtually no chance of ever paying off their loans. The less-obvious answer is that even people who are eligible for solid mortgages with respectable interest rates and competitive monthly payments are lured into less-suitable mortgages based on appealing but dangerous low monthly payments. The catch? Lower is not necessarily better when it comes to monthly mortgage rates. In reality, lower is not necessarily even lower. Let me explain.

Prospective homeowners' poor mortgage decisions coupled with unscrupulous and predatory lending were a leading cause of the 2008 subprime mortgage meltdown. Home buyers were offered mortgages that weren't good for them, and their utter lack of awareness caused them to make poor decisions. Of course, the lenders are also to blame, but this isn't about blame. This is about equipping yourself with the knowledge you need to avoid making poor decisions when it comes to buying or financing your home. Fortunately, you can learn from the mistakes of others.

Hundreds of thousands of people signed mortgage contracts that promised the lowest monthly payment available, unaware that these loans were toxic for them (and for the economy, as it turns out). In many cases, these loans were suggested by a home builder or mortgage lender who was trying to convince someone to buy a house they couldn't afford. (We'll address the affordability of housing on Day 51). All blaming aside, borrowers could have—and would have—avoided these mortgages if they had known more about them. In the paragraphs that follow, I'll take you through the various types of mortgage loans available in order to help you make the best choice and eliminate your risk of falling prey to a shoddy, exploitative mortgage in the future. For now, here are the types of mortgages to steer clear of.

Four Mortgages to Avoid

1. **Interest-Only**
   This type of mortgage only requires you to pay the interest on your loan for a period of time, not to pay down the balance of the loan. When this interest-only period of your loan eventually expires, you either have to refinance your loan or pay off the balance if full. This type of loan was incredibly popular from 2000 to 2007 until the real estate market took a beating. Because you don't begin paying off the money you actually borrowed until you've paid off the entirety of your interest, you also don't increase the equity in your home (which is what makes buying a house a valid investment) unless real estate prices rise. When real estate prices

fall, on the other hand, you are immediately "under water." In other words, you've actually lost money.

2. **Adjustable-Rate Mortgages (ARM)**

   An adjustable-rate mortgage begins with a fixed interest rate, but at the end of its introductory period, the interest rate adjusts to match market rates. Let's say you have a 5/1 30-year ARM. This means that you will have a fixed interest rate for the first five years. After the five-year introductory period, your rate is subject to an increase to the going market rate. It's not unusual for an interest rate to rise at least 2% in that time. It might not sound like much, but it could be devastating to your financial situation.

3. **2-1 Buydown**

   This mortgage program allows you to pay a fee to lower your initial monthly mortgage for two years. This was (and still is) a very popular tool in new home construction. Many home builders don't particularly care whether or not you can afford a home in the long term. Their main concern is selling you a home now, and they are willing to pay a fee, known as a *buydown fee*, in order to lower your monthly payments for the first two years. Whether or not you can afford the house two years from now when your mortgage increases is of no concern to them, they simply want to shift the burden of responsibility to someone else. But it should concern you. Remember, you should never rely on the financial advice of someone who's trying to sell you something.

4. **No-Money-Down**

   The primary feature of this type of loan is pretty self-explanatory: you can buy a house without putting any money down. I hate to be the bearer of bad news, but if you can't afford a down payment, you can't afford a house. True, you may be able to afford the monthly mortgage payment, but you can't afford to be a homeowner. The only thing worse than wiping out your emergency reserves to make a down payment on a home is buying a home without any emergency reserves to speak of in the first place. You're only a paycheck or two away from disaster.

Mortgage brokers and the new-home construction industry have made a fortune by convincing consumers they should buy homes with no money down. You've probably even seen late-night infomercials that encourage you to start a no-money-down real estate empire, but I adamantly disagree that this is ever a good idea. (In general, it's safe to assume you don't need anything sold on late-night cable channels.)

Here is my fundamental point: you want to secure favorable mortgage terms so that you don't feel obligated to explore any of these types of loans.

If you've already fallen victim to one of these types of mortgages or your mortgage rate is higher than average, you're probably thinking, "Thanks, Peter, but this advice is too little, too late." I thought you might say that, so for the rest of Day 13, I'm going to explain the key to regaining control of your monthly payments and to solidifying your position as a homeowner: refinancing.

Refinancing is the process of securing a lower interest rate on your mortgage, either by finding a new bank to handle your mortgage loan or by renegotiating with your current lender. Don't make the mistake of thinking that this is something you can put off or avoid. If you currently own a home (and are paying a monthly mortgage), you should consider it a valuable asset whose management is just important as that of any other investment.

When dealing with your real estate assets, focus primarily on how they're financed. You'll need to answer the following three questions to decide whether or not refinancing makes sense for you:

1. **Is my interest rate significantly higher than current mortgage rates?** You can find current mortgage rates by going to your mortgage or bank website. Many people are so busy that they don't realize how much money they could be saving by taking advantage of lower interest rates. If interest rates are favorably low, take the time to explore refinancing your mortgage. For that matter, it always pays to have a general awareness of mortgage interest rates.

2. **Does the cost to refinance my mortgage make sense in the long run?** To determine whether refinancing makes sense in the long run, consider the following: say that refinancing your house will save you $200/month, but it will cost you $3,500 to do so. This means that it will only make sense for you to refinance if you plan to live in your house for at least 18 months. Otherwise, the refinancing process will do nothing to improve your financial standing. Having a trusted mortgage advisor to talk to is very important since he or she will let you know if refinancing is worth the cost. Great, but how do you find a trusted advisor? (On Day 47 we'll discuss what you should look for in a financial advisor.) For now, start with a referral from a family member or friend who had a positive experience with their own mortgage broker.

3. **Do I even qualify for a new mortgage?** In order to qualify for a mortgage, you need to have a steady income, to have relatively good credit (based on the lending environment) and owe no more on your house than it is worth (which might not be the case if you opted for one of the four mortgages we just discussed). When your home is worth less than what you owe on it, this is called being "upside down" or "underwater." This is not a good financial position to be in. Being "underwater" will preclude you from refinancing and from many other financial opportunities. Homeowners who are "underwater" frequently struggle with money management.

If, after asking yourself these questions, you decide to explore refinancing, here is how to do it:

1. **Call your current lender** and ask about their "streamline" refinance program. A streamline refinance allows you to refinance with your current lender with few qualifying factors. Your interest rate changes but little else does.

2. **Call a mortgage broker.** A trusted mortgage broker will inform you of the current interest rates and qualifying criteria. You can also see if better rates are available than those being offered through your current lender's streamline refinance program.

3. **Weigh the options.** If you can save at least .75% (just under 1%) on your mortgage or you can make up for the cost of the refinancing within 18 months, do it. This will help free up cash flow for your other financial priorities. As with all refinancing options, make sure you are staying in your current residence long enough to take advantage of the savings.

   As a general rule, a savings of .75% will make refinancing worthwhile, but there is always more to take into account, which is why I can't stress frequently enough how important it is to have a trusted mortgage broker.

4. **Go forth and refinance.** If you determine that refinancing is appropriate for you, submit an application to the new lender detailing all of your assets, liabilities and income. An underwriter will evaluate your application and decide whether you are a good credit risk. Once you receive approval, a closing date will be set and you will sign your name about five million times (okay, maybe not, but you will sign your name quite a bit). Finally, you'll start making payments under the new terms to the new lender. It's a slightly complicated process, but it is worth it.

PETE SAYS:

Take the time to compare your mortgage rate and terms to what is currently available. Saving .75% of interest on your mortgage can make refinancing worth it, but only if you are planning on staying in your house for thee to five years or more.

> Information is power. You cannot possibly make informed financial decisions without it. You don't always need to know exact current mortgage rates, but you do need to be aware of how the current economy can benefit or harm your personal economy.

I recently worked with a married couple who were in the midst of an absolute financial meltdown but who were able to resolve their financial problems by refinancing their home as described in this chapter. Chad and Emily were the perfect example of "when it rains, it pours"—and an example of how a little bit of resourcefulness can save the day.

The trouble started when Chad's hours were reduced at work and Emily had to begin making payments on her student loans after having deferred them for as long as she could. At the same time, their car insurance bill increased by $50 per month. Needless to say, they were looking for something—anything—that would help them stanch the financial bleeding. They decided to review their biggest asset and their biggest liability. In this case, their biggest asset, their house, *was* their biggest liability. Our solution was to contact a local mortgage broker to see if they could refinance their 7.5% 30-year mortgage. At the time, the current mortgage interest rates were less than 5.75%, meaning that they were able to save over $380 on their monthly mortgage payment simply by refinancing. This freed up cash and allowed them to adequately deal with their financial challenges.

Day 14

Resist the Urge to Take the Easy Way Out

At first glance debt consolidation programs might seem like a great cure-all. For a simple fee—about 10% of your debt—you can enroll in a program that will handle all of the mechanics of paying off your debt. Sounds like a pretty sweet deal, right?

Well, it's not. It's a very bad deal. Debt consolidation is bad news for a number of reasons. And as you might have guessed, I'm going to give you all the gory details.

"Paying off debt may not be fun, but it's a beautiful struggle."

Eliminating this struggle by enrolling in debt consolidation programs (or falling prey to other such gimmicks) puts you at risk of also eliminating the chance to gain good financial habits from the debt-payoff process. Because we're focusing on developing healthy financial habits that will remain with you long after your debt is history, it's important that you avoid the various financial traps out there. Debt consolidation programs top that list. It's the debt equivalent of a get-rich-quick scheme: promising in the short term but bound to bite you in the behind somewhere down the road. And, as you can imagine, these programs are unreliable and flawed.

Let's look at three common debt consolidation misconceptions:

1. **Debt consolidation programs make paying off debt painless and easy.**
   Sure they do. That is, if you consider financial ignorance painless and easy. Debt consolidation lowers your interest rate and your monthly payment, but significantly increases the amount of money you owe and prolongs the time it takes to pay it off. Imagine, your laziness and unwillingness to address poor financial decisions will finally be addressed by...*your being lazy and unwilling to address poor financial decisions!* Your goal is to get out of debt quickly, yet when you choose debt consolidation you acquire more debt and it takes longer to pay off.

2. **Debt consolidation wouldn't be allowed if it weren't good for you.**
   Of course it wouldn't. Neither would drinking, skydiving or smoking. The assumption that debt consolidation is somehow benevolent is common, but it couldn't be any further from the truth. The U.S. economy operates with free markets and free choice. That means debt consolidation programs can freely exist even though they capitalize on poor financial choices.

3. **Debt consolidation won't hurt my credit score.**
   Are you sure about that? As you learned in Week Two, raising or preserving your credit score shouldn't be your primary financial goal. One of the side effects of being financially savvy is that your credit score will practically become an afterthought. But in case you still insist on making it a priority, yes, debt consolidation can (and often does) hurt your credit score. Debt consolidation companies negotiate with your creditors to reduce your debts. The debt consolidation company sets up a trust account for your monthly payments. This trust will ultimately be used to pay off your debt in an agreed-upon amount. The debt consolidator, however, doesn't pay your credit card bill until the trust account has enough money to pay off the debt in full. As a result you will begin or continue to get harassing mail and phone calls

from creditors, and you will damage your credit score until there is enough money in the trust account to pay off your debts. (If you're already getting calls and/or mail from creditors, see my "Three Steps to Communicating with Creditors" on the next page.)

Long story short: debt consolidation is a terrible choice. A good budget paired with a debt-reduction plan (like the one I outlined earlier this week) is all that you need to get out of debt. Sure, it will take a little bit more time and dedication, but you'll develop invaluable habits along the way, avoid paying outrageous fees to people who prey on poor decisions and avoid further potential damage to your credit.

If your creditors are already sending you threatening letters or calling you endlessly, you need to act now.

To do this, you are going to act as your own personal debt consolidation agent. I know this might sound confusing, considering I've spent the last couple of pages railing against these people, but bear with me here. In theory, debt consolidation is simply the process through which one makes payment arrangements that differ from "normal" payment terms, and there is no reason you can't benefit from this process by setting up such terms for yourself. So, rather than paying someone a premium to do it for you in a way that does not benefit you, you can take matters into your own hands by arranging payment terms that you can afford at no additional cost. I suggest doing this only if you have copious debt or are behind on payments.

Taking the following three simple steps will help you get back on track by communicating directly with your creditors.

Three Steps to Communicating with Creditors

1. **Call the collection agency and inform them of your intent to pay.**
    You might be surprised how far this small gesture can go.
    There are two things you should do when you make this call.
    1) Start the conversation by telling the credit agent, "I'm calling to
    make arrangements to pay off my debt." This sets a proactive
    and cooperative tone for the conversation. 2) Lose the attitude.
    Creditors might not be the most uplifting people to talk to, but
    this situation isn't their fault, it's yours. You want to establish an
    excellent rapport with the collection agent since he or she will
    be making decisions that affect your financial future.

2. **Be willing to suggest a reasonable payment schedule.**
    This is where negotiation comes into play. Yes, you can negotiate
    how much you're going to pay back. In fact, collection agents are
    encouraged to make deals with you. They're compensated based
    on how much they collect from you. And trust me, your paying
    them something (on a scheduled and regular basis) is better than
    your paying them nothing as far as the representative is concerned.
    But don't get carried away. You aren't doing them a favor. You
    owe them money and are simply fulfilling your obligations.

3. **Do not miss a payment after you agree to a payment schedule.**
    You are ultimately at the mercy of your creditors. They can and
    will void any previous arrangement if you fall behind again. And
    then you'll be right back where you started.

You can communicate directly with your creditors in a much more efficient
and cost-effective way than you would by hiring a debt consolidation
company. I urge you to resist the temptation to take the easy way out.
You'll regret it, and you can do better on your own equipped with the tools
described above.

Week Three

Control Monthly Spending

If your ultimate financial goal is to have more disposable income, you have two basic choices: you can make more or you can spend less. In an ideal world you would do both, but let's face it, many people make the mistake of choosing only the former and end up living from paycheck to paycheck as a result. This crucial mistake is the product of a harsh reality: increasing your income to accommodate your spending habits is much more difficult than bearing down and spending less.

This week, we're going to take the road less traveled, which is also the high road. You're going to learn how to spend less money. There is quite possibly no nobler process. It almost brings a tear to my eye. But I won't get mushy on you just yet. We have work to do.

Day 15

Understand the Abundance Mentality

Whether intentionally or accidentally, many people experience manufactured financial tranquility thanks to too much money in their checking accounts. While this may sound like a good problem to have, it can be a very dangerous one for a couple of reasons. For one, a checking account has a very low yield, meaning your money is only gaining minimal interest when it could instead be working for you. But more importantly, and less obviously, it can ruin a perfectly good financial situation.

Let me explain by using my favorite resource—toilet paper—as an example. As unpleasant as it is to think about, we've all been faced with the very alarming prospect of being stranded without the appropriate amount of toilet paper. And by stranded, I mean truly stranded. There are no other rolls at your disposal, and you must survive on whatever is left on the roll. Sure, it's humorous to think back on now, but it's extremely unfunny in the moment. The point is, faced with the cardboard, you will survive in any way possible, and you'll learn two lessons because of it: 1) Check supply levels *before* you use the bathroom! 2) Scarcity does not have to mean going without—it simply requires you to be more resourceful to get the results you want. It's easy to be wasteful when you have a full roll and to forget what you went through when faced with an empty one. Abundance is the enemy of resourcefulness, and sometimes you need scarcity in your life to regain the balance.

The same thing can happen when you have a relatively large roll, er, balance in your checking account. This feeling of financial abundance can occur with as little as $100 or $200 "extra" in your checking account. The amount of money that causes this strangely damaging phenomenon is different for everyone. It all depends at what amount you start to be relatively complacent.

Think about your checking account. At what point do you stop checking the balance in your head before making a purchase? When you have a cushion of $100? $200? $500? When you become comfortable with your cushion, your economic stress eases, and you start making spending decisions that aren't always prudent or even practical. This is what I like to call "abundance spending." Or a feeling of financial comfort that leads you to buy items normally out of your price range for the very simple fact that you know you *presently* have the money to cover them.

This is why a feeling of financial abundance—whether manufactured or legitimate—can be dangerous. The larger the cushion you give yourself, the larger the financial mistakes you can make. If you need evidence, think about all of the celebrities and once-well-off public figures who've gone bankrupt. When you hear these stories, you wonder how someone who once had so much could now have next to nothing. I'm not a betting man (but you probably already knew that), but I'd guess that in 99% of these cases, abundance mentality played a very large role.

Of course, the abundance mentality isn't limited to celebrities (or toilet paper, for that matter). I see it all of the time in my in-the-trenches personal finance work. In particular, I recently worked with a woman who had a pretty pronounced problem bouncing checks—something I wholly credit to her refusal to hold herself accountable for her spending. After months of reckless spending and high overdraft fees, she devised a solution: she would transfer the $3,000 she normally kept in her savings account to her checking account. This way, she wouldn't have to worry about incurring overdraft fees on her checking account when she carelessly overspent. While this transfer certainly eliminated the overdraft fees, it didn't get to the root of the problem, which was her spending habits *not* her overdraft fees. By transferring "extra money" into her account, she was simply putting off having to face the problem at hand. Worse, not only did her "solution" not work, but it created a whole other problem: She spent the $3,000 that she transferred into her checking account without even thinking about it. Clearly, this was no solution. We ultimately had to dismantle her reliance on this cushion, and we worked to address the real problem (her spending) instead of the scapegoat (the overdraft fees).

Today, you're going to eliminate the abundance mentality from your personal financial situation.

Here's your challenge: Take your checking account balance below $100, and keep it there for one week. Of course, if this is the normal state of affairs for your checking account, this won't be a difficult task. And if keeping your checking account balance at $100 presents a struggle because you don't usually even have that much disposable income available to you, today's lesson is simply that having a bigger checking account balance doesn't necessarily reduce the amount or severity of financial problems. As Notorious B.I.G. so eloquently phrased it, "Mo' Money, Mo' Problems." But for those who keep money in their checking accounts when they'd be better off putting those funds toward paying down debts or making investments, this can require quite a bit of discipline, which, as you might have already noticed, is a recurring theme throughout this 60-day challenge.

The benefits of this exercise?
- You will learn financial restraint.
- You will train yourself *not* to spend money to solve everyday problems.
- You will become accountable for your spending.
- You will increase your overall awareness.

Awareness is key here. Very often it's our financial passivity that keeps us away from our financial goals.

For those of you who will be reducing your balances for this exercise, know that there's nothing wrong with having a small checking-account balance. It will teach you to be more responsible for each purchase you make, and that's an incredibly powerful skill to have.

Control Your Abundance Mentality. As I mentioned, your goal is to keep your checking account balance at $100 or less for one week. But there are some guidelines you need to consider along the way:

1. **You can't spend your way down to $100.** The idea is not to get rid of money for the sake of getting rid of money. It's a matter of putting it to better use, whether by paying bills or making it work for you more efficiently.

2. **You don't want to complete this exercise when you have outstanding checks.** Doing so could cause your balance to go negative when these checks clear.

3. **Account for any automatic withdrawals you have scheduled during this period.** Make sure your $100 balance is independent of any pre-set automatic payments. If the total of these withdrawals will cause your account to fall into the negative, do not participate in this exercise at this time. There are two approved ways of getting your balance down to $100 or less in this exercise:

    1. **Pay any open bills you have—utilities, rent, credit, family loans, you name it.**
        You may find that you're able to put a sizeable dent in some of your bills by letting go of the need for comfort money. You might even be able to use this exercise as an excuse to pay off a long-standing

bill—one for which you've been prolonging full payment in order to maintain a cushion in your checking account. Now that you know that this practice isn't particularly effective, give yourself permission to pay it off once and for all. Being debt-free is one of the most satisfying financial cushions out there.

2. **Transfer your excess money into savings.**
   If you've paid all of your open bills and still have a checking account balance greater than $100, transfer the remaining money into a savings account. If you don't have a savings account, there's no better time than now to open one. While a savings account isn't a long-term strategy for putting your money to work for you, it's a far better option than keeping extra money in a checking account. This is for one very simple reason: saving accounts offer interest. Interest rates differ by bank and by state, but free money is free money, no matter how you look at it. Just make sure you're aware of any time limitations and restricting stipulations put forth by your bank. Some banks require you to commit to keeping money in your savings account for a specified period of time, some have minimum balances and others penalize you for too many transfers between checking and savings. You want to find a savings account that makes sense for your situation and supports your reasonable personal goals.

The point of this exercise is to illuminate the importance of every single transaction you make in a single week. When you keep your checking account balance to a minimum, your financial decision making is not at risk of being tainted by an abundance mentality. Instead, you'll learn to function with a scarcity mentality. Just as manufactured financial tranquility can make you feel unjustifiably at ease with your finances, manufactured financial scarcity can trigger financial survival mode. By keeping excess funds in your account, you leave yourself open to some potentially disastrous spending decisions. Why take that risk?

Day 16

Master the Grocery Store

Believe it or not, the grocery store is a microcosm of the world at large when it comes to spending decisions. In this microcosm you can isolate certain behaviors and decision-making processes, analyze them and then use the resulting data to alter your financial behaviors in all spending situations. Do you make impulsive purchases? Are you easily distracted by shiny and sparkly items? Or do you stick to your grocery list? These are the type of questions you will consider when assessing your grocery store habits.

Good decisions at the grocery store benefit you in two ways.

1.   They can directly and positively affect your finances in specific areas of your life:

   •   By planning meals based on what's on sale and in season, you can reduce your impulse buying, overspending and food waste.

   •   You can decrease your health-care costs by making proper food choices.

   •   If you can become immune to catchy but often meaningless grocery store marketing tactics (such as flashy packaging and strategic shelf placement that appeal to your sense rather than your needs), it's likely these discretionary skills will carry over when you face similar tactics elsewhere.

- Saving at the grocery store means more money to distribute among other areas of your budget. Not only can you put this money toward your larger financial goals, you can commit it to those items in your budget that are leaner on funds. Often these items are things like entertainment and dining out.

We'll get into more detail about each of these later in this chapter.

2.   Savvy grocery shopping can help you develop the following good habits that will carry over to all financial decisions:

- Frugality
- Willpower
- Strategic planning and execution
- Prioritizing
- Budgeting and problem solving

If it seems like I'm putting a lot of pressure on your trip to the grocery store, that's because I am. No doubt you consider these trips a means of picking up food for dinner, but they play a key part in a much grander financial plan. Think about it. When you walk through a grocery store, one particular concept is abundantly clear: choice. You could buy anything you want, but should you? You could look for deals, but will your love of great packaging and your tendency to notice only those products that are at eye-level trump your need for a good bargain? You could buy brand names, but generic is cheaper and not that different (if at all) from brand-name items. Ultimately, your most important choice is whether to spend excessively to act on your compulsions and to get instant gratification or to save money and develop good habits that will benefit other areas of your life. With the goal of achieving the benefits identified above, you should focus on the nine best ways to save significantly at the grocery store. The skills you develop won't just help you navigate the aisles, they'll help you in all aspects of your financial life.

1. **Shop with a list.** The best way to cut back on impulse buys is to purchase only what's on your list. Your goal at the grocery store should be very simple: never be surprised by what you put in your cart. A good list will make your trip purposeful and organized. The trick, of course, is putting the right things on your list in the first place—items that will deliver the best value. (Flavor doesn't hurt, either.)

2. **Don't go grocery shopping when you're hungry.** We're all fully aware of this logic and we even agree with it, but many of us still don't heed the warnings. The fact of the matter, though, is that when we go to the grocery store hungry we end up leaving with a bunch of items that satisfy our current cravings but don't necessarily meet our rational grocery needs. This is because hunger is a survival instinct that has the power to trump logic. Combine survival instincts with cravings and clever grocery store marketing tactics, and, well, there goes your carefully-planned list (and sometimes your diet). Even worse, many times we don't finish eating the impulse items we buy and end up wasting the food altogether.

3. **Buy generic whenever possible.** Only buy name-brand products when it's absolutely necessary. You can save as much as 40% when you buy store brands instead of name brands, and in many instances the store brand is actually manufactured on the same production line as the name brand. A *Consumer Reports* study of 65 grocery products revealed hardly any differences in quality between store-brand items and national name-brand items.[1]

4. **Stick to the outer aisles and departments of your grocery store.** The way most grocery stores are laid out, customers will discover the most value and fewer processed foods around the periphery, where you commonly find the produce, meat, fish and dairy departments.

---

[1] Source: *"Consumer Reports'* ® Tests Find Quality of Store Brands' Products on Par With National Brands," www.ConsumerReports.org, July 2005.

5. **Cut out the junk food.** Calorie-rich junk food may be cheaper than nutritious snacks in the short term, but the savings actually come at the cost of your long-term health. A 2009 study suggests that obesity costs the United States health care system an additional $147 billion per year in health care costs.[2] And don't forget about high blood pressure, high cholesterol and various ailments caused by vitamin and mineral deficiencies. Cut out junk food to preserve or improve your health because the simple fact is that a poor diet is more likely to bring about the health problems that can cost you a lot of money down the road. If you're like many other Americans, kicking the addiction to junk food might be one of your toughest challenges, so don't feel compelled to do it all at once. Start by cutting out one item at a time: this week, chips; next week, chips and soda; and keep working at eliminating junk food from your grocery store regimen until those unnecessary items (and calories!) are out of your system. You will be amazed by how much you save in the long run.

6. **Shop for what's on sale.** To find out what's available, visit your supermarket's website and develop your weekly menu accordingly. Don't plan your week's menu simply based on what you want; plan it according to sales and values. (The good news is that, many times, these two things overlap.) Let's say you feel like making pork chops one night, but you discover that pork tenderloin is on sale at $3 less per pound than pork chops. Most people don't really care what form that porky flavor comes in, so why not opt for the tenderloin and save? A menu based on what's on sale can translate into significant savings at the grocery store over time. You just need to have a flexible palate...*and a little imagination.*

7. **Shop for what's in season and available locally.** The high demand for out-of-season and non-native produce, such as avocados during the winter in the Midwest, fuels producers' willingness to supply

---

[2] Source: *Health Affairs*, July 27, 2009.

them, but this supply comes with a hefty price tag. And it should. Think about the resources necessary to ship your avocado from Chile to Ohio: manpower, gas, time, international trade taxes and other logistics of transportation. Similarly, take a quart of in-season strawberries. They may cost you $2.99 in July when they are in season, but the same quart out of season can cost you as much as $5.99. Do you really need fresh strawberries in December? Do they even taste that good then? Maybe it's time to dig out that apple crisp recipe. Buying food that's in season and local to you drastically reduces these costs, producing savings that are reflected at the checkout counter.

8. **Look for your protein sources in alternate forms.** Relying solely on meat as your primary source of protein can become expensive quickly. You can get plenty of protein by eating more beans, nuts, seeds, eggs, and leafy green vegetables. Need inspiration? Look to Mexican and Indian cuisines for ideas on how legumes, vegetables and grains can be transformed into serious flavor without meat.

9. **Look around.** Competing food brands are constantly battling to get premium placement on grocery store shelves. This means that the brands that end up at eye level are often those with bigger budgets, and because of this, they're often more expensive. Similarly, if you have kids, they're likely to be drawn to the purposefully kid-friendly packaging of the items placed at their eye level. Make a point of looking at the products above and below these two target shelf-positions. Who knows? You might just see a bargain.

These days, grocery shopping can pose serious challenges for shoppers who want to eat healthfully and stick to a strict budget. Additionally, many people want to purchase food from organic sources, which can be pretty expensive. If eating organic foods is important to you, you need to factor that into your budget as a priority, which will likely mean de-prioritizing something else.

Pop Quiz: Grocery Store Behavior

You didn't think I'd give you all of that good information without quizzing you on it, did you? Take a minute to answer the following questions, and let's see how you check out!

Yes No

---

1. ☐ ☐ Do you clip (or download) coupons?

2. ☐ ☐ Do you have a predetermined grocery budget?

3. ☐ ☐ If you answered "yes" to question #2, do you stick to your weekly grocery budget when at the store?

4. ☐ ☐ Do you use a grocery list?

5. ☐ ☐ Does your list include budget-friendly pantry staples like rice, pasta and canned vegetables that you can rely on to shape meals?

6. ☐ ☐ When leaving the grocery store, does your cart contain fewer than three items you hadn't planned on buying?

7. ☐ ☐ Do you buy generic brands when they are available?

8. ☐ ☐ Consider your food waste: do you use items in your refrigerator rather than letting them acquire a layer of green fuzz?

9. ☐ ☐ It's 10:00 p.m. Do you know what's in your fridge? (Can you list the major items on the shelves?

10. ☐ ☐   An overstuffed fridge can mean wasted money.) If you have children, do you have a system in place to avoid being waylaid by racks of candy and other tempting treats that stores place at kid-level near the checkout lanes?

11. ☐ ☐   Do you tend to stick to the outer aisles and departments of your grocery store?

____ ____   **Total**

If you answered "Yes" to seven or more questions, you are a disciplined shopper who has developed the kind of restraint and analytic skills required for smart saving and budgeting. You can resist the pull of the frozen-waffle aisle—most of the time, anyway.

If you answered "No" to five or more questions, it's time to change. Commit to using the tools and strategies offered in Day 16 to conquer your grocery-store demons and create substantial savings.

Going back to the notion of buying organic for a moment, the most health-conscious client I ever had was a woman named Bridget. She took care of herself and her family by being committed to nutrition, and she stocked her house with copious amounts of fresh and organic food. As a result, she spent nearly $1,500 per month on groceries for a family of four. This was devastating to her family's financial situation, as her spending on groceries was getting in the way of her plans to save for retirement or for her children's education, not to mention those plans to pay off her own lingering student loans. But she didn't care. *I cared.*

Here was an otherwise disciplined individual who lost all reason the moment she touched a grocery cart. Her refusal to understand the logical limits of her grocery habits bled into other areas of her financial life. She justified most of her spending by claiming that she only wanted the best for her family. But she was using her hopes for her family's health to justify poor decision-making.

She got so carried away with her grocery shopping that she didn't even take the time to look at any cost-cutting measures. Her family's health was important to her, but that didn't mean that she had to bludgeon her finances to maintain it. Bridget and I sat down and incorporated many of the nine strategies above into her grocery-shopping methods.

The most significant step for Bridget was her creation a weekly meal plan. She had been stocking her pantry and fridge with items she knew she might not use. As a result, her kitchen had evolved into a mini grocery store where she could essentially "shop" whenever she needed to. While that might sound wonderful, it was incredibly inefficient and expensive. Her lack of planning for the week was also leading to waste, especially when it came to perishable foods (such as produce, meat and poultry). So our strategy revolved around teaching her exactly how to project which items she would use. (Needless to say, her first few weekly meal plans included a variety of healthy meals involving many of those extra ingredients she had already stockpiled in her kitchen.)

The lesson Bridget learned is that you can't mask your unwillingness to make decisions simply by invoking your concern for your family (or making other such excuses). In the end, the simple act of sitting down to make a weekly menu allowed Bridget to cut her grocery budget by 40% while continuing to maintain a healthy diet for her family.

Day 17

Dining Out

Not only is dining out convenient, it's fun. There's no shopping for hard-to-find ingredients, no lengthy preparation and perhaps best of all there's no clean-up. Unfortunately, if you don't have a grasp on how dining out affects your financial life, you could be in for a great deal of trouble, long after you pay the bill.

Sixty-six percent of American adults say they dine in a restaurant at least once a week.[1] Our love for dining out is further illustrated by the National Restaurant Association's 2009 Restaurant Industry Forecast, which projects that American restaurants will make over a half trillion dollars in 2009. [2]

Figures like these no doubt result in large part from our hectic work schedules. If you're a member of the great American rat race like I am, it's easy to accept that sometimes a person simply doesn't have the time or the energy to go grocery shopping and prepare adequate meals. Also according to the 2009 Restaurant Industry Forecast, over 69% of American adults claim to visit restaurants to simplify their lives. Of course, if you're working incredibly long hours just to sustain dining habits that are meant to

---

[1] Source: "Eating More; Enjoying Less," Pew Research Center, April 19, 2006.

[2] Source: "2009 Restaurant Industry Forecast," National Restaurant Association®.

simplify your life, you might be in the middle of a nasty cycle. And if you're just a workaholic, that's a completely different issue altogether! You might be thinking, "Gee, Pete, the reason I work so hard is because I want to eat out all of the time. I do it because I enjoy it, not because I'm too busy." Good point. To many people, dining out is not only a source of sustenance, it's a primary source of entertainment. Both of these situations are common and fair. But no matter how you look at it or what your position is on the matter, you should be fully aware of how dining out affects your personal bottom line and the array of financial decisions you're confronted with each time you do it.

Most of us are very passive when dining out because it's such a commonplace occurrence. The goal of this chapter is for you to learn how to become a more conscious diner by being more aware of the small financial decisions you make when you dine out. We'll also determine just how much you spend eating out each week and month. This way, you'll be equipped to make informed decisions every time you enter a restaurant.

Let's start by reviewing how much you spend each week dining out. Warning: This is going to be tedious but very revealing.

COFFEE
How many days per week do you buy prepared coffee drinks (as opposed to preparing your own)? _____

On average, how much do you spend on each coffee drink? $ _____

Multiply these two numbers. This is your Current Weekly Coffee Expense.
Formula:
Number of prepared coffee drinks per week: _____
x   Average amount spent per coffee: $ _____
=   Current Weekly Coffee Expense : $ _____

BREAKFAST

How many times per week do you eat breakfast out? _____

On average, how much do you spend on each breakfast out? $ _____

Multiply these two numbers. This is your Current Weekly Breakfast Expense.

     Formula:

     Number of breakfasts eaten out per week: _____

x   Average amount spent per breakfast: $ _____

=   Current Weekly Breakfast Expense : $ _____

LUNCH

How many times per week do you eat lunch out? _____

On average, how much do you spend on each lunch out? $ _____

Multiply these two numbers. This is your Current Weekly Lunch Expense.

     Formula:

     Number of lunches eaten out per week: _____

x   Average amount spent per lunch: $ _____

=   Current Weekly Lunch Expense : $ _____

DINNER

How many times per week do you eat dinner out? _____

On average, how much do you spend on each dinner out? $ _____

Multiply these two numbers. This is your Current Weekly Dinner Expense.

     Formula:

     Number of dinners eaten out per week: _____

x   Average amount spent per dinner: $ _____

=   Current Weekly Dinner Expense : $ _____

COCKTAILS/ALCOHOLIC BEVERAGES

How many cocktails or other alcoholic beverages do you purchase each week when dining out? _____

On average, how much do you spend on each cocktail/alcoholic beverage? $ _____

Multiply these two numbers. This is your Current Weekly Cocktails/Alcoholic Beverage Expense.

Formula:

Number of cocktails/alcoholic beverages purchased while dining out per week: _____

x   Average amount spent per cocktail/alcoholic beverage: $ _____

=   Current Weekly Cocktail/Alcoholic Beverage Expense : $ _____

OTHER BEVERAGES

(This includes any non-coffee or non-alcoholic beverages, other than tap water, purchased while dining out.)

How many beverages do you purchase each week when dining out? _____

On average, how much do you spend on each beverage? $ _____

Multiply these two numbers. This is your Current Weekly Beverage Expense.

Formula:

Number of beverages purchased while dining out per week: _____

x   Average amount spent per beverage: $ _____

=   Current Weekly Beverage Expense: $ _____

DETERMINE YOUR CURRENT MONTHLY DINING-OUT EXPENSE

How much do you typically spend on dining out each month?

To determine your total Monthly Dining-Out Expense, add together your weekly coffee, breakfast, lunch, dinner, cocktails/alcoholic beverages and other beverage expenses, and multiply this number by 4.33 .

Formula:

Current Weekly Coffee Expense: $ _____

+   Current Weekly Breakfast Expense: $ _____

+   Current Weekly Lunch Expense: $ _____

+   Current Weekly Dinner Expense: $ _____

+   Current Weekly Cocktail/Alcoholic Beverage Expense: $ _____

+   Current Weekly Beverage Expense: $_____

=   **Current Weekly Dining-Out Expense: $_____**

Current Weekly Dining-Out Expense: $_____

x   4.33 (average number of weeks in a month)

=   **Current Monthly Dining-Out Expense: $_____**

DETERMINE THE PERCENTAGE OF MONTHLY INCOME SPENT ON DINING OUT:

Next, you are going to determine what percentage of your monthly income you are spending on dining out. To do this, divide your Current Monthly Dining-Out Expense by your Net Monthly Income.

Formula:

Current Monthly Dining-Out Expense: $_____

/   Net Monthly Income: $_____

=   Percentage of Monthly Income Spent on Dining Out: _____ %

Are you shocked by this number, or is it roughly what you expected? Do you consider this number high or low? What percentage of your monthly income does it represent?

In general, you should be spending no more than 6% of your monthly income on dining out. This percentage represents a different amount of money for everybody because everybody's monthly income is different. Also, keep in mind that this percentage might be unfairly low for people who allocate much or all of their entertainment budgets to dining out.

If you've determined your Monthly Dining-Out Expense to be too high (greater than 6%), it doesn't mean you should never eat out. While this very well may be the case for some people, most of us can significantly reduce our Monthly Dining-Out Expense by being more conscious of our dining habits, by altering them to account for wasteful spending and by making informed decisions. This could mean lowering the frequency with which you eat out, altering the types and quantity of dishes and beverages you order or choosing different restaurants altogether. As a result of simply raising your general awareness while dining out, you'll transform into an active, rather than a passive, diner. And that alone is half the battle.

Here are 10 valuable tips for dining out without turning your wallet inside out:

1. **Determine your meal budget before you go out to eat.**
   This can be a monthly budget or a per-meal budget. Either way, the idea is to set aside a limited amount of money each month based on the 6% benchmark and not to spend a penny more.

2. **Take advantage of special offers, promotions and discounts.**
   Restaurants occasionally offer special promotions such as early-bird or happy-hour specials. I've seen some marketing-savvy restaurants offer customers coupons for signing up for email newsletters, exclusive deals to members of their various social media communities and even "passwords" to their online followers. Also, keep an eye out for age-specific discounts. If you're a senior citizen, many restaurants will offer you a discount as long as you show identification. It's important to let your server know that you'd like to take advantage of these discounts, though, since they aren't always automatically applied to your bill. Check out restaurant gift-certificate websites. It's not unusual for restaurants to offer steep discounts online, such as a $25 gift certificate for $10 (though you should be sure to read the fine print for qualifications and expiration dates).

3. **Take advantage of prix-fixe (fixed price) dinner menus.**

   Often restaurants will offer a three-course meal (appetizer, entrée and dessert) at a reduced rate. While your menu selection may be limited, you can indulge in three courses (and sometimes even drinks) at a relatively lower price. This is a smart way to avoid the tyranny of many separate à la carte charges, which can add up quickly.

4. **Keep your alcohol intake and bar tab down.**

   Have you ever ordered your favorite bottle of wine—say a reasonably-priced cabernet—at a restaurant, only to find that it costs $45 more than the $15.99 you normally pay for it at the store? That's because restaurants and bars typically mark up wine approximately 300%. And the markup on liquor at some restaurants and bars can be over 400%? Take your glass of wine. The price you pay for a single glass may be the same as the price the restaurant paid for the entire bottle.

   I can't tell you how much money I've saved by having a drink with my wife at home before dinner and then sticking with water when we dine out. In metropolitan areas where drinks can run between $10 and $15 a pop, cocktails can double or triple your bill. Think about your dining experiences or even happy hour out with your friends. How much money would you save if you limited yourself to one drink with dinner? Savor your beverage. When you do, you will be able to toast a lower dinner bill.

5. **Limit your consumption of non-alcoholic beverages.**

   Sure, non-alcoholic beverages like juices, teas, milk and hot chocolate are a lot less expensive than their alcoholic brethren, but the markup on these drinks is exorbitant. And many times, people order certain drinks out of habit rather than any real desire (a good example of this is ordering orange juice with breakfast). If you're really craving a certain drink, try to limit yourself to one per meal, and remember that not all drink refills are free.

6. **Consider buying a coupon book.**
   The next time the neighborhood kids come around selling entertainment coupon books for a school fund raiser, flip through the book and see if there are coupons for restaurants you're interested in. You might find a few good surprises.

7. **Consider splitting an entrée.**
   Have you seen portion sizes lately? Even if the restaurant charges a fee to split the entrée (usually about $3), this is an instant way to save—and believe me, you won't leave hungry.

8. **Get a doggy bag.**
   If you're dining alone, get half of your meal boxed up for a hassle-free (and cost-free) lunch the next day.

9. **Consider going to lunch instead of dinner.**
   Have you ever noticed that your favorite restaurants have dinner items you love on their lunch menus, too? And at half the price? That's because they know people are accustomed to paying more at dinner. Replacing your dinner date with a lunch one is one of the best ways to derive value, and restaurants that might be out of your price range for dinner often have very reasonable lunch menus.

10. **Plan ahead by looking at menus online.**
   Now that you can find practically everything online, look up restaurant menus for places you plan to visit. Previewing these can make you a knowledgeable consumer.

Dining out can be a form of entertainment and should be accounted for as such. But dining out due to sheer laziness or perceived convenience is destructive to a planned financial life. Can some of the money you spend dining out be redirected toward your financial priorities? Of course it can. And even minor changes in your dining habits can lead to savings.

Day 18

Lower Your Utility Bills

How much attention do you give to your utility bills each month? If you're like most Americans, probably not much. Most of us glance at the totals, roll our eyes at the seemingly endless taxes and then pay the bill because we don't think there's much we can do about it. But that's where we're wrong.

We tend to take the cost of "fixed" bills like these for granted. But are utility bills really fixed? Not really. Your habits, knowledge and overall awareness can affect them, and you can reduce your utility costs with very little effort. The tactics we'll explore today have been known to free up to $300 from the annual budgets of those who go through the *60 Days to Change* program. What do you say? Would you tweak a couple of your habits if it meant freeing up $300 per year? I thought you would.

The same discipline you use in other areas of your financial life can be applied to reducing your utility expenses. Without a real grasp of their traditional utility bills—gas, electricity, water and so on—the majority of Americans have begun justifying the addition of new fixed expenses as well. As we discussed on Day 6, the New Necessities have become life fixtures much in the same way as the *real* necessities. The average American has upwards of six or seven fixed expenses each month, including utility bills. I'm not going to make the case for getting rid of things you consider necessities—although you should certainly consider it if you're in debt—but they can add up and drain your checking account if each expense isn't monitored intently. Perhaps the first question you should ask yourself is whether or not all of your necessities are, in fact, necessities. We'll get to that, though.

Today, you're going to take the time to explore the various money-saving programs your different utility providers offer (but don't always go out of their way to advertise). Can you bundle your different services? Can you switch to budget billing so you don't have seasonal spikes on your bill? Does your water company offer an incentive for you to switch to low-flow shower heads and toilets? You can easily answer these questions by calling your utility providers and/or visiting their websites.

At their websites, familiarize yourself with their different payment options. Compare those options to the amount you pay monthly. Are you spending more than you need to in order to get the services you need? If so, make changes if they will ultimately save you money, and then watch the savings happen over the next few months.

You need to manage your utility bills in the same way you manage your assets. Since changing your financial life is all about changing your habits, adopt the following money-saving and energy-saving habits:

1. **Consider installing a programmable thermostat.** This allows you to be energy efficient when you're away from your home during the day. If you don't have a programmable thermostat, settle on a temperature a few degrees lower (during winter) and higher (during summer) than you're used to. You'll be surprised by how much you can save.

2. **Turn off the lights when you leave a room.** This is such an easy and obvious way to conserve energy and save money, yet many people don't do it. This tactic should be applied outdoors as well as indoors. There's no need to keep lights on in unoccupied rooms, just as there's really no reason to light your front lawn or backyard at night. If you're concerned about intruders or that people won't be able to find their way in the dark, consider switching to motion-detecting lights. These simple changes can lead to significant savings over time.

3. **Conserve water.** Even if your water company doesn't offer an incentive to adopt water-conserving strategies, the potential financial savings should be incentive enough. Low-flow shower heads, aerated faucets and "float boosters" in the toilet tank are great ways for homeowners to lower their water bills.

4. **Unplug appliances and other devices that use energy when not in use.** This includes your television, toaster, cell-phone charger and your hair dryer. Also, turn off surge protectors and power strips when you're not using the electronics plugged into them. Keeping these items plugged in wastes energy and money.

5. **Do you really need a cell phone *and* a home phone?** Sometimes a new necessity like a cell phone can replace a traditional one entirely. Many people no longer need a land line but keep it because they don't want to get rid of a phone number they've had for years. The way I see it, paying the phone company a fixed amount every month simply for the privilege of having a sentimental phone number and a service you can live without is a lot more painful than the steps you can take to get replace your home phone with your cell phone once and for all. If you already have a cell phone and are ready to make the switch, start by emailing your contacts your new number. Next, put your cell-phone number on your land-line voicemail or answering machine for a month prior to turning off your home phone service. Finally, personally call those whom you want to have your new number (and skip over those you don't!).

6. **Check for air leaks around windows and doors; seal cracks and drafty spaces.** Why spend time and money heating or air conditioning your home if the air is escaping through cracks? The principle of preventing waste alone should motivate you to investigate your home's efficiency. Saving money is icing on the cake.

7. **As your mother probably said, "If you're cold, put on a sweater."**
   If you're in a region that relies on heating oil or natural gas in the
   winter, your heating bills can fluctuate as the commodity prices of
   these resources change. You can beat this (even if only temporarily) by
   putting on another layer and resisting the urge to turn up the heat.

These steps may seem minor, but the small things truly do have the largest
effects. From my experience, making these changes can save you as much
as $300 per year. That's $300 you can use for your real financial priorities.

My client Gabe's story clearly illustrates how these tactics can save money.
He's a counselor and summertime landscaper who has always had budgeting
problems. During the winter, his problem is particularly pronounced: heating
costs stretch his paycheck so thin that he ends up with multiple overdraft
charges. But because his job is weather-dependent, his income is higher during
the summer (and his heating bills are obviously lower as well). So his real issue
here isn't budgeting but timing. Well, timing *and* awareness. When I met with
him, he admitted that he had never taken the time to consider how his utility
bills could be affected by his habits and decisions—he had just come to accept
winter high-heating bills as a fact of life.

The solution? At my urging, he took five minutes to contact his natural
gas provider and signed up for their budget-billing program. The program
distributes heating costs evenly throughout the entire year's bills and
allowed him to pay a consistent amount each month. So instead of having
his bill fluctuate between $50 and $400 each month depending on the
season, he now pays a fixed fee of $150 per month. This fixed bill didn't
eliminate any of Gabe's debt per se, but it did make it easier for him to
budget year round, which drastically improved his ability to focus on his
financial goals and the other areas of his budget that needed attention.

Day 19

What's Your Vice?

This entire week you have been learning how you can change your buying habits in order to improve your financial life. So far we have mainly discussed "necessities," but it is also imperative that you address your pleasure spending. A life stripped of all pleasure is hardly the point of *60 Days to Change*. In my experience financial programs that ask you to give up everything fun simply aren't effective. Your goal is to form healthy financial habits, and choosing *one* indulgence is part of this. Today, you will own up to your financial vices, but identify the one you just can't quit.

There's nothing wrong with having a favorite indulgence or a guilty pleasure. A vice only becomes a problem if you wear a white suit and start hanging out with a guy named "Tubbs." We call this a Miami vice. (Sorry, I couldn't help myself.)

The non-Miami type of vice is classically defined as "a weakness in character," but for our purposes we'll be lenient and define it as "an admission of the importance of moderate frivolity." I doubt that every dime you spend goes towards "the necessities" in life. We all spend money to attain pleasure, so I want to face this admission with the gravity and respect it deserves.

I'll start with my personal vices: dining out and nice clothes. While I enjoy both of these things, enjoying them simultaneously on a regular basis would easily drive me to the poorhouse. I've learned to make choices and to enjoy things in moderation. When it comes to vices, there's no need to be compulsive or excessive (because these two traits are what transform an innocent vice into a bad habit), but it's not always easy to keep your vice(s) in check. My solution is to spend money on my vices on a seasonal schedule. For example, I usually shop for clothes only in the spring, which allows me to satisfy my desire to dine out a number of times throughout the rest of the year.

It's worth noting that just because you have a strong desire for something doesn't mean that you have to spend absurd amounts of money on it. I like nice clothes (beyond what I would consider necessities), but my favorite belt only cost me $6. And I love good food, but the same is true of price and quality there, too. Price and quality aren't always or even frequently synonymous, although clever marketers have successfully convinced the nation otherwise. But I digress. The bottom line here is that satisfying a vice isn't always about spending (unless, of course, the very act of spending *is* your vice). Many times, indulging your vice can simply mean allowing yourself to focus on something that you enjoy. Because all work and no play, makes… Well, you get it.

Since the word vice is traditionally used to describe things that are socially taboo, it's sometimes difficult to get people to admit theirs—even to themselves. But the truth of the matter is that vices can be healthy—that is, like anything else, in moderation.

(On that note, excessive gambling, drinking and smoking are some of the old tried and true vices. But because I like to emphasize good health, sound habits and good decision making, I don't endorse focusing your hard-earned money excessively on these habits. But then I don't endorse excessive *anything* during this exercise. Whether you choose to indulge in some of these more unhealthy vices or in perfectly healthy ones, please remember the cardinal rule of moderation. My lawyer and your posterity thank you.)

Let's take a look at a vice that exemplifies "moderate frivolity."

A friend of mine claims that her vice is ordering grass-fed meat online from a very specific farm in Missouri.[1] She doesn't make a ton of money but with the spare money she does have, she indulges in having this meat shipped to her, rather than just walking down the street and buying it from the local butcher.

A vice is not defined by the frequency of its occurrence.

My friend says she orders meat about every other month, which is hardly excessive.

A vice isn't always, or even usually, rooted in logic or rationality; it's often an emotional or irrational treat.

My friend is fully aware that having specialty meat shipped to her across the country is not the most cost-effective way of getting it (although she would argue that it's really not much more than what she pays at the store). She also knows that she can easily get grass-fed meat locally, but her brief explanation is that she likes the company and that the meat tastes great.

Fair enough. As long as her financial life is in order—which it is—it's not my place to argue this one. It's her vice, and I'm going to let her have it.

Which brings me to my point: why try to fight all of your financial vices? *60 Days to Change* isn't about sacrifice; it's about making smart decisions and spending in moderation so that you can live comfortably. Having

---

[1] In case you're wondering: U.S. Wellness Meats (www.USWellnessMeats.com)

a number of unwieldy, expensive or out-of-control vices doesn't fit that description. If that's what you're looking at as you review your vices, your job today is to choose your favorite vice and to learn to control it. Only then can you begin to think about factoring another into your budget.

Pick a vice, any vice.

You can't have the best of all worlds, so what's it gonna be?

(Hint: If you have to think about it, then it's probably not your vice. But just in case you need some help getting your wheels turning, I've taken liberty of listing some of the all-time classics below.)

- Cars
- Home decorating
- Shopping
- Dining out
- Beer/Wine/Alcohol
- Hobbies
- Exercise
- Music
- Movies
- Travel
- Technology
- Pet(s)
- Socializing (Read: Drinking with friends)

You may look at these things and think to yourself, "My car isn't a vice; it gets me to and from work every day. You know, so I can support my family. That's what I consider a necessity!" Or, "Exercise isn't an indulgence, Pete. You've been talking about the importance of good health throughout this entire book and now you want me to reconsider my exercise schedule. What gives?"

These are fair and common reactions to this list. The important thing to consider here is that these items aren't vices unless people choose to make them so. A Chevy Impala, for instance, might not seem like a vice to your average car enthusiast, but if the cost of buying it is disproportionately high compared to your income, it's a vice. Likewise, a monthly gym membership is great as long as it's a membership you can afford. Can you realistically be a member at the gym with the rooftop pool, or should you settle for the one without? These are the types of decisions you must consider when reviewing your vice(s).

That said…

"My vice is _____.
But that doesn't mean I can go crazy with it."

NOTE: By don't "go crazy," I mean don't obsess over your vice. Don't spend all day shopping online to obtain it. Don't empty your emergency fund to satisfy it. And don't, under any circumstances, put your vice on a credit card. This is supposed to be a fun and realistic exercise. Don't ruin it with fits of crazy.

How much should you spend on your vice?

At the end of any given month, if you've saved enough to have a surplus in your account after you've tended to all of your bills and obligations, you're free to spend a reasonable amount of that surplus on your vice. (You will learn all about surpluses and shortages on Day 24.) Therefore, the bigger your monthly surplus, the more you can spend on your vice. But you must make sure that you address your financial priorities first.

Here's how I would recommend determining how much to allot to your vice:

Once you've started making regular contributions to your emergency reserve and retirement accounts (Day 37 covers retirement accounts in detail), you can spend up to 50% of your surplus on your vice. This figure, however, should not exceed 5% of your net monthly income. For example, if you take home $4,000 each month, the amount of money you spend on your vice should not exceed $200:

Net Monthly Income x 5% = Your Vice Budget

So, $4,000 x 5% = $200.

Or to be even more specific, let's say that your surplus for the month is $500. That means that 50% of your surplus is $250. Even so, you're going to want to cap your "vice budget" at $200 (or 5%). Why? Because while you want to reward yourself for your hard work and discipline, you also want to make sure that you dedicate enough of your surplus to your other financial priorities, such as debt, short-term savings and long-term savings. Just because you've tended to your monthly commitments doesn't mean you've satisfied all of your financial goals.

If I have money left over after bills at the end of the month (a surplus), the most I can *afford* to spend on my vice each month is (Net Monthly Income X 5%): $ _____.

You've just identified another reason to operate on a lean budget. The bigger the surplus, the more you can spend on your (healthy) vice. Enjoy!

Day 20

Don't Overcommit to Monthly Payments

How many monthly bills, invoices and automatic checking-account withdrawals do you have? Although it probably seems high, Americans, on average, commit to about 10 fixed monthly bills to sustain their lifestyles. Among these bills are such standard expenses as utilities, car payments, mortgage (or rent) payments, credit card payments and insurance. It starts getting slippery when your monthly commitments creep above these accepted standards—and when "reasonable" monthly payments become a justification for the affordability of frivolous purchases. Depending on the person, I can sometimes make a case for up to 15 fixed monthly bills, but anything over that is out of control, no matter how you look at it.

Which begs the question: Do you have more than 15 fixed monthly bills? If so, I can tell you two things with almost complete certainty: 1) you're over-complicating your life, and 2) you're committing to something you can't afford. Just because you can afford the monthly payment, doesn't mean you can afford the purchase. Today, you will address your number of financial commitments.

The Cost of Living.

It might seem high but the average American pays about 10 bills each month. Here are 15 common fixed monthly expenses. How many of these expenses do you claim each month?

1.   Mortgage/Rent
2.   Gas
3.   Electricity
4.   Water
5.   Waste
6.   Car payment
7.   Car insurance
8.   Health insurance
9.   Phone
10.   Cell phone
11.   Cable
12.   Internet
13.   Life insurance
14.   Credit card(s)
15.   School loans

As we discussed in Week Two, companies allow you to pay them on a monthly basis because purchases seem more affordable that way. Think about it: Would you sign up for a cell phone if you had to pay $1,400 up front for the first year? Would you lease a car if the company required you to pay a $4,000 lease fee in one giant chunk? How about $1,200 for cable? The answer is probably not. But when those expenses are spread out over a year, the total of the purchase can seem like a lot less than it actually is.

Do you justify your purchases by breaking down the purchase price into monthly payments like these? If you've ever watched late-night TV, you've no doubt heard the phrase "three easy payments," which was created to help you make bad buying decisions. Ask yourself if you really need the things you're trying to justify buying. ("Self, do I really need the Snuggie™?") And take a second to multiply the cost of one of these "easy payments" by three. Can you afford it? At this very minute? I've seen many financial lives filled with and ruined by "easy monthly payments." The ironic thing is that the more "easy" payments you have, the more *difficult* it becomes to keep up with them.

"The phrase "three easy payments" was created to help you make bad buying decisions."

We've all agreed to small monthly payments outside the normal utility and credit-card bills at one time or another, only to later regret the toll on our finances. For example:

- $50/month to have your lawn mowed
- $10/month for a satellite radio subscription
- $11/month to lease a water softener
- $15 - $20/month for a newspaper
- $100/month to have someone clean your house
- $30/month for bottled water delivery
- $10/month for identity-theft protection
- $30 - $100/month for a gym membership
- $25/month for a coffee-of-the-month club
- $100/month for music lessons
- $10/month for movie subscriptions

The list goes on...

None of these items seem expensive on its own. When combined, however, they cost between $391 and $466 per month, or $4,692 and $5,592 per year. But my bigger concern is really the justification of this kind of spending. Before you commit to a long-term repeat purchase, do the math. How much does a year's worth of this item cost? Can you really find room for it in your budget? If so, will it require you to remove something else? I'd hate to tell you not to introduce your children to instruments as a cost-cutting measure, but you might need to get a cheaper gym membership and mow the lawn yourself in order to make room for lessons in your budget. And along the same lines, which of these things can you live without in order to send money toward your larger financial goals?

> **NOTE:** If you're a parent, you might be thinking that your minimum number of fixed monthly expenses should be higher than that of someone without dependents. On the one hand, you're right; it's expensive to have children. On the other hand, this logic tends to get many parents in financial trouble. They begin viewing their purchases for their children as separate from the household expenses as a whole, and sometime even justify a set of 10 new expenses for their children. But this just doesn't make sense. After all, which of the above expenses don't cover your children's needs at the same time they cover yours? Unless you're paying your children's rent or they have a separate electricity bill, your minimum number of monthly payments should be very similar to that of someone without any dependents (albeit your average bill is likely much higher). I'll be lenient, though—I'll give parents one extra fixed monthly expense per child. I'd hate for them to miss out on piano because of me.

The real problems begin when you don't realize how many monthly commitments—no matter how small—you have. Remember that a big part of being successful financially is raising your general level of awareness so that you can make informed decisions. Going into this exercise, many people have five to 10 extra monthly bills due to past indiscretions and too many instance of committing to *easy monthly payments.*

How many monthly payments are you obligated to pay each month?

List your monthly commitments and the amount of each in the table provided below.

Item	Yes	No	Amount per month
Rent or mortgage	☐	☐	$ _____
Electricity	☐	☐	$ _____
Gas	☐	☐	$ _____
Water	☐	☐	$ _____
Waste	☐	☐	$ _____
Car payment (including monthly lease fees)	☐	☐	$ _____
Credit card #1	☐	☐	$ _____
Credit card #2	☐	☐	$ _____
Phone	☐	☐	$ _____
Internet	☐	☐	$ _____
Cable	☐	☐	$ _____
Health insurance	☐	☐	$ _____
Student loans	☐	☐	$ _____

Yes	No	Item	Amount per month
☐	☐	Personal loans	$ _____
☐	☐	School tuition	$ _____
☐	☐	Newspaper subscription	$ _____
☐	☐	Magazine subscription	$ _____
☐	☐	Video-rental subscription	$ _____
☐	☐	Gym membership	$ _____
☐	☐	Maintenance fees (homeowner, lawn and landscaping, etc.)	$ _____
☐	☐	Music lessons	$ _____
☐	☐	Sports lessons	$ _____
☐	☐	Coffee of the month	$ _____
☐	☐	Identity theft protection	$ _____
☐	☐	Other _____	$ _____
☐	☐	Other _____	$ _____
		Total:	$ _____

How'd you do? If you have more than 10 to 15, you need to reevaluate your buying habits. How? First off, avoid signing up for any more "easy" monthly payments. Next, determine which of these monthly payments you can eliminate. I should stress that this is not a question of whether or not it's possible—it's not only possible, it's necessary. The question is exactly *which* fixed expenses to ditch, and which financial goal to focus on with the money you free up as a result.

And no more easy monthly payments!

Day 21

Eliminate Overdraft Fees

You probably have a line of credit with your bank but don't even know it. But don't get excited. It has a variable interest rate that sometimes reaches upwards of 1,000%. Yes, this dubious line of credit has a name: *overdraft protection.*

Overdraft protection might not seem like a credit line at first blush, but that's exactly what it is. Essentially, when you withdraw more money than is available in your checking account, the bank gives you a loan to cover your payment to the payee (thus helping you save face rather than letting on that your account's balance is negative). Sounds great, right? Here's the catch: the interest rate on this loan is exorbitantly high.

According to the *Financial Times,* financial institutions are projected to make over $38 billion this year on overdraft fees.[1] That's hardly chump change. It also means they're not in a hurry to help you find ways to avoid incurring these fees (though they may have to if Congress passes legislation to protect consumers from overdraft fees). Furthermore, banks have employed some less-than-ethical techniques to increase the number of overdraft fees you might have, via a tactic called *reordering.* Reordering

[1] Source: "Banks make $38 billion from overdraft fees," *Financial Times,* August 09, 2009

means that the bank clears your debit card and check transactions in descending amount order, so larger transactions clear first while smaller ones fall to the bottom of the list. So, if by some chance you have miscalculated and spent more than is in your account, the bank has the system rigged to make it more likely that you won't just get hit once. Nope, you'll get hit with an overdraft fee for each little charge. You might have only overdrawn by $20, but since your small purchases got bumped to the bottom of the list, you're now paying an overdraft fee on your cup of coffee from Starbucks *and* your gallon of milk from the supermarket *and* that bag of dog food from the pet store. Ouch. Pretty dirty trick, isn't it?

Banks describe their overdraft protection programs as a "courtesy" service they provide customers. You should be so lucky to have other "courtesies" like this in your life. Overdraft protection can turn a $2 cup of coffee into a $37 cup of coffee overnight. Now that's some serious appreciation. But I don't blame the bank in this scenario.

I blame you.

Under what circumstances does an account trigger overdraft fees? When there isn't enough money to cover what you spent. Who balances the supply-and-demand ratio on your checking account? You do. So, not to mince words, it's your fault.

Sure, I could give you some tips on how to reduce your overdraft fees, but that's not getting to the root of the problem. I want you to eliminate your overdraft fees by either monitoring your spending more closely or by disallowing overdraft fees as an option on your account. The latter is quite simple: turn off your overdraft protection by calling your bank's 800 number and asking the customer service representative to turn off your overdraft protection. You can also manage your account online or go into a physical bank branch and speak with a representative.

Now that you no longer have overdraft protection, you're no doubt wondering what's going to happen when you spend more than you have in your account. The answer is that you won't—the bank won't let you. Instead, they allow you to get declined. Sometimes publicly. Yep, the consequence of not having overdraft protection is the gut-wrenching phenomenon known as credit declination or, in the case of a check, a bounced check. I don't know if you've ever had your card declined, but let me tell you, it's jarring. So jarring, in fact, that I'm convinced people should go through it just so they can see their financial lives flash before their eyes. I'm certain they would come out of it as better people.

This is my long way of saying, yes, it is better to have your card declined publicly than to pay exorbitant overdraft fees. Yes, it can be embarrassing, but the alternative is to allow your bank to play fast and loose with your money. Better to take matters into your own hands—even if it is through a jarring and unnerving, "Sir/Ma'am, I'm sorry, this card has been declined." Or better yet, go a step further in taking charge of your finances, and keep your spending in line with the money available in your account. Whatever path you choose, your first step must be to turn off your overdraft protection today—that way these exploitative bank loans won't even be an option next time you're careless in your spending.

Week Four

Budget Week

You're probably surprised that it took me this long to tackle the budgeting discussion. Many financial programs have you jump head first into budgeting. But not this one.

When you don't take the time to develop your financial acumen before you create your budget, you are more likely to fail. In order to set up a workable budget—and to be committed to following it—you need to know what's at stake for you financially. I hope by now, after working through the previous 21 days, you have the financial insight and context you need to tackle the most important part of your new financial life: your budget.

Days 22 through 25 will teach you specific tactics that will allow you to set up, maintain and make financial decisions based on your budget. The rest of the week will show you how to apply your new knowledge to the financial world at large.

Day 22

Create a Monthly Budget

The art of living on a budget sometimes gets a bad rap. It's often confused with penny-pinching and can seem very limiting to outsiders who are lucky enough to observe their fiscally-responsible friends' financial precautions. But no matter on which side of the budgeting table you sit, I want you to throw out any negative associations you have with the word budget—thrift, economy, scraping, penury—and replace those loaded concepts with three new ones: awareness, communication and accountability.

Awareness
A lack of financial awareness can crush you whether you make $30,000 a year or $300,000 a year. A lack of awareness is the primary reason people continue to live paycheck to paycheck even as their incomes increase. Budgeting is the process of making yourself consistently aware of your needs and your spending, and done right, it can take you from a paycheck-to-paycheck lifestyle to one with the luxury of financial security.

Communication
In addition to causing lifestyle challenges, financial irresponsibility is one of the most common causes of stress and conflict in relationships. A lack of communication about monetary issues is historically responsible for lovers' quarrels, fights, break-ups and even divorces that could have been avoided with open, honest discussion.

Picture this. You open the mailbox and sort through the normal junk mail, catalogs and bills you get on a daily basis. Among them, you see your monthly credit card statement. You open it and find that… What? She/he spent how much?! You have just discovered (or are once again confronting) the unsavory spending habits of your partner. Usually the "conversation" that follows this scene is full of loud voices, accusations and red faces.

I'm not a relationship counselor by any stretch of the imagination, but when it comes to finances' ability to affect relationships I can assure you that regular communication—under less volatile and surprising circumstances—can do wonders. On Day 27, we'll talk about budget meetings, which are meant to drive communication between you and the person/people with whom you share financial responsibilities.

Accountability

Along with awareness and communication, you should factor accountability into your new budgeting vernacular. The act of holding yourself accountable for your actions is important in any situation that involves working toward a goal, and if your goal is to change your financial life for the better, you must face your financial decisions head on. The concept of accountability is often the most difficult of the three in that it requires you to be both the judge and the judged. In other words, not only are you setting goals for yourself, you're also critiquing your ability and efforts to meet them. This means constantly facing your harshest critic—you!—and being honest when you do.

The Budget

A monthly budget is a tool that allows you to introduce all three of these concepts into your financial life. It should be the centerpiece on your financial table.

Your budget needs to be, in one word, simple. And it must allow you to accomplish three things: understand your shortcomings, objectively analyze your spending and make strategic changes to your habits as a result. The sample budget that I provide will familiarize you with some of the more common categories found in personal or family budgets. Within each category are the related expenses. The columns will allow you to compare your spending projections with your spending reality. Here's a breakdown of the type of information that will be included in each column:

Column 1: Categories and Expenses. List each of your monthly expenses in the category that makes the most sense.

Column 2: Price targets. Price targets are the spending limits you assign to each item in your budget. You will learn how to establish price targets on Day 25, at which point you will return to complete this column.

Column 3: Actual spending. List the actual amount you spent on each item at the end of the month for comparison with the planned cost in Column 2.

Column 4: Difference. This is where you will note the difference between each item's projected and actual cost. To do this, subtract the number in the "Price Target" column from the number in the "Actual Spending" column. In this case, a positive number is actually a bad thing. It means you spent more than you budgeted. A negative number, therefore, means you spent less than you projected.

(Actual Spending) – (Price Target) = Difference

Feel free to use this sample budget as the basis of your own. Your budget doesn't need to be any more complicated than this.

Tip:

Creating your budget in a spreadsheet will make your calculations much easier.

Category/ Expenses	Price target	Actual spending	Difference
Housing			
Mortgage/Rent			
Electric			
Natural gas			
Phone			
Cell			
Internet			
Waste			
Water			
Lawn care			
Homeowners association/ co-op			

Category/ Expenses	Price target	Actual spending	Difference
Transportation			
Car payments			
Gasoline			
Maintenance			
Auto insurance			
License plates			
Public transit			
Food			
Groceries			
Coffee			
Dining out			

Category/ Expenses	Price target	Actual spending	Difference
Beverages			
Personal			
Clothing			
Dry cleaning/ laundry			
Hair care			
Medical			
Books/ subscriptions			
Entertainment			
Gifts			
Pets			

Category/ Expenses	Price target	Actual spending	Difference
Debt Payments			
Debt #1			
Debt #2			
Debt #3			
Debt #4			
Savings and Life Insurance			
Tier 1: Short-term savings			
Tier 2: Mid-term savings			
Tier 3: Long-term savings			
Life insurance			

*Many people dedicate an entire category to entertainment, but I always include it as a single item within the "Personal" category. The way I see it, if you view entertainment as something that needs its own category with multiple items, you will likely spend a lot more money on it. Try thinking about entertainment as part of your personal (psychological!) care routine for now and see if and how that affects your spending.

Day 23

Find the Surprise Bills

Nothing sends an otherwise smoothly-sailing financial ship reeling quite like an unexpected bill. The funny thing, though, is that most unexpected bills are not surprises at all, just financial commitments that have been forgotten. Some of the most common examples of these obligations are car-insurance bills, license-plate renewals, vacation bills and holiday expenses—all of which are frequently, but most often unintentionally, left out of personal budgets.

On Day 23, we're going to identify some of the more common of these oft-forgotten periodic expenses and translate them into monthly or annual entries in your budget.

"Surprise" expense	Annual costs	Monthly costs	Where this item fits within my budget
Car insurance			
Homeowner's/ renter's insurance			
Vacations			
License-plate renewals			
Car mainte- nance			
Landscaping			
Tuition			
Veterinary bills			
Clothes			
Property tax			
Birthday and holiday spending			
Income taxes			

Did the items in this table remind you of others that you've accidentally overlooked? If so, add those in as well. You might also need to add columns to account for expenses that occur weekly, quarterly, bi-yearly and so on.

From there, plug these new items into your main budget in the category you identified in the right column of this table.

And just like that, you're all done for today. *Really*. Sometimes it doesn't take a whole lot of work to replace financial surprises with financial awareness.

Day 24

Track Monthly Surplus and Shortage

One of the main reasons for maintaining a monthly budget is to determine whether the previous month produced a shortage or a surplus. Just as every business in the world should know whether the previous month produced positive or negative earnings, individuals should be aware of their own monthly peaks and valleys. Not knowing where you stand each month could lead to serious financial hardship. It's time to start thinking of your household—or at least the financial parts of it—as a business.

Remember, there's nothing wrong with having neither a surplus nor a shortage if you've met all of your financial obligations for the month. This simply means you have done a good job budgeting.

"Yes, Pete," you're saying. "I know what surpluses and shortages are. Can I skip this day?" NO! Today, we're going to go beyond simply knowing what they are; we're going to explore how you should be thinking about them in terms of your *60 Days to Change* and how you can apply them to your overall financial strategy. The good news is that we're going to get through all of that rather quickly.

Surpluses

At risk of stating the obvious, surpluses result from not spending all the money you've made in a given month. A surplus is the amount of money left over after paying all of your bills and allocating money to the investment/savings categories you've identified in your budget: emergency fund(s), a savings account, life insurance and/or other investments. Assuming you've met these monthly obligations, a surplus opens you to opportunity. It's a powerful tool that can and should be used to accomplish your longer-term financial goals.

So what should you do with it?

The best three ways to use a surplus are:

1. **Pay off debt.** This means going above and beyond the monthly payment you set for yourself on any outstanding balances.

2. **Save the money for an upcoming "expensive" month.** Many times, surpluses are fleeting rather than regular. If this month's surplus is a one-off—maybe due to a bonus or monetary gift—the best thing to do is set the extra cash aside for a less fortunate month or even for a surprise bill you didn't account for despite your better efforts.

3. **Put the money into long-term savings.** If you've paid off your debt and you can safely say that this surplus will be consistent and representative of your financial situation for months, even years, to come, it's time to get serious about your long-term savings. On Day 43, we'll talk about monthly automatic savings—something that might be a good option for you. And if it's something you're already taking advantage of, consider increasing your monthly deposits.

If you consistently have a surplus, yes, you can be slightly more lenient with your spending.

Shortages

Shortages occur when you spend more than you make. This situation has happened to everyone at one time or another, but it shouldn't happen all the time. There will be months during which you'll pay for a vacation, buy gifts or pay a six-month insurance premium. If you've planned it right by forecasting upcoming surprise expenses in exercises like the one you completed on Day 23, however, you will have offset and pre-fund these expenditures by putting money aside in less demanding months. Even though you will have spent more than you made during that particular month, you won't fall into a shortage situation.

There are two types of shortages: anticipated shortages and surprise shortages.

Anticipated shortages

A semi-annual recurring payment, such as an insurance payment, is an example of an anticipated shortage. You know you are going to spend more than you make in this particular month, but since you have saved money for that payment over the previous months, you are able to head off a shortage crisis.

Surprise shortages

Surprise shortages occur when your spending exceeds your income due to something you haven't anticipated, such as an emergency or uncontrolled spending. In the case of an emergency, it is fair to consider the shortage an isolated occurrence, and you should take the months after the emergency to systematically replenish your funds. If, on the other hand, careless spending led to the shortage, it's important to identify your point of weakness and then use the methods introduced last week to gain control and avoid a similar situation in the future.

By identifying surpluses and shortages as part of your monthly budgeting regimen, you'll always know when you can apply excess funds to debt or savings and when you need to show more restraint in spending to prepare for less abundant months. These are the tell-tale signs that you are mastering your financial situation and increasing your financial awareness once and for all.

I'm starting to get a bit sentimental about it all, really...

Day 25

Establish Price Targets

By now you've made it through some of the most challenging aspects of budgeting—namely, airing your credit card-statement dirty laundry and tackling surprise spending that can cripple your budget. The next step? Setting the parameters that will help you regulate your spending in all areas of your life.

Price targets are the spending limits you assign to each item in your budget. Essentially, establishing price targets is a fancy way of describing the act of setting individual budgets for each item on your budget based on your monthly obligations and income. Think of price targets as "mini-budgets."

If you refer back to the sample budget I provided at the end of Day 22, you'll see that price targets comprise column two. Your goal is to keep your monthly spending less than or equal to the target amounts you set for each item in order to keep your overall monthly budget on track. Done correctly, price targets allow you to create several small victories every month.

Establish price targets
1. Start by calculating the three-month spending average for each expense item in your budget. Averages are essential here as it is difficult to change your monthly spending—let alone figure out what a reasonable

amount is—if you don't have the context of a monthly average gathered over time. Don't try to set price targets using just one month's data. You'll end up with skewed numbers.

Note that some items in your budget are fixed, such as your car payment and your rent or mortgage. Go ahead and enter those fixed costs as the price targets for the corresponding items. When you pay off a car loan or other such finite expense, you can then take the money you budgeted for that item and put it towards savings.

2. After you've calculated the average for each item, reduce each one by 10% to identify your price targets. Why 10%? Well, simply put, people tend to waste money. So much money, in fact, that the vast majority of us can reduce our spending by 10% without feeling a thing. For some, however, reducing spending by 10% still won't be enough to eliminate overspending altogether. The point of this exercise is to reduce your spending, which will get some people to their optimal monthly spending levels and others at least a little bit closer.

   By cutting each item by 10%, you are simply trimming the fat around your price targets rather than cutting into your needs. Think of it as streamlining your spending.

   Don't freak out if the reduced numbers don't seem realistic. You'll find that by applying the habits we've developed over the last three and a half weeks, meeting these goals is a lot easier than you ever thought possible. Sure, it will take some time, but you'll get there by remaining consistently focused and dedicated.

Let's take a look at the simple calculations involved in establishing a price target by examining a sample grocery budget.

Add your total spending on groceries for the last three months:
Month 1 ($500) + Month 2 ($300) + Month 3 ($400) = $1200

Determine your average monthly grocery costs by dividing this number by three:
$1200/3 months = $400 per month

Multiply your monthly average by 10%:
$400 x 10% = $40

Reduce your monthly average by 10%:
$400 - $40 = $360

Your price target for monthly groceries is $360, which means that your goal is to keep your monthly grocery spending at or below $360. (For concrete strategies on how to become a smarter, more efficient shopper in order to stay within your price target, revisit Day 16.)

Price targets help you reduce spending because they break your spending into manageable, digestible increments. While you might have trouble keeping track of how your grocery trips fit into your overall budget, you should find it less daunting to keep track of them in relation to your monthly grocery budget.

One reason you've taken the time to establish your price targets is so that you can address them objectively during your monthly budget meetings. (We'll discuss budget meetings on Day 27.) Once a month, you will compare your actual spending to your price targets as a means of tracking your discipline and your progress toward your financial goals. Even better, if you spend less than your price target, you'll improve your chances for an overall monthly budget surplus.

Now it's your turn.

Before we continue on to Day 26, try determining the price target for an item in your own budget. Let's look at your average monthly entertainment spending, for example. Plug your costs into the formula to determine your price target:

Add your total spending on entertainment for the last three months:
Month 1 ($) + Month 2 ($) + Month 3 ($) = $_____

Determine your average monthly entertainment costs by dividing this number by three:
$[total entertainment spending]/3 months = $_____ per month

Multiply your monthly average by 10%:
$[average monthly entertainment costs] x 10% = $_____

Reduce your monthly average by 10%:
$[monthly average] - $[10% of monthly average] = $[your entertainment price target]

Your new monthly price target for entertainment is $_____

It's crucial to constantly strive to improve your price targets. If you come in under your price target three months in a row, it's time to lower the target another 10%. The more often you come in under the price target, the more quickly you'll meet your financial goals.

Day 26

How Do You Stack Up?

The *60 Days to Change* program is designed to drive personal progress, but sometimes there's benefit in measuring personal progress against existing trends. The idea is not to set benchmarks for yourself based on what everyone else is doing; rather, this knowledge will help you maintain a general awareness of where you fall relative to others. Are your efforts placing you among the average Joes or ahead of the pack? Assuming you're taking your *60 Days to Change* seriously, I won't even suggest that you're lagging behind the norm.

Today, we're going to take a look at how your financial situation stacks up in comparison to your peers—that is, in comparison to the rest of the country.

Take a look at the national personal spending averages below. These figures are from the most recent U.S. Bureau of Labor Statistics Consumer Expenditures Study (2008).[1]

Purchase Category	Percentage of Gross Income
Food	12.8%
Clothing	3.6%
Housing	33.9%
Entertainment	5.6%
Medical	5.9%
Transportation	17.0%
Other	21.2%

Because I spend so much time analyzing consumer expenses, I have some observations about the above percentages that I think are worth sharing.

1. It's fair to assume that the "Other" category, which occupies over one fifth of the average American's budget (21.2%), includes items such as gifts, savings, debt, pets and the hundreds of other things that don't fit into the more standard categories listed above it. With all of these entities merging into just one category, it's doubtful that the average American is saving as much money as he or she should (a minimum of 10% of gross income, which we will discuss more in Week Seven). In other words, it's unrealistic to think that Americans are putting half of their "Other" budgets toward one goal (savings) and the other half towards several (everything else).

2. Over one third of the average American's gross income is spent on housing expenses, meaning that a budgeting or spending mistake in this area could spell disaster for even the most stable financial plan.

---

[1] Source: "Consumer Expenditures in 2008," U.S. Bureau of Labor Statistics. http://stats.bls.gov/cex/home.htm

3. Americans spend a tremendous amount of money on transportation, most of which goes toward the standard expenses of owning a car (monthly payments, maintenance, gas and insurance). If you live in a city with good public transportation options, you have a significant opportunity to save money.

4. The average American spends 12.8% of his or her gross income on food. By diving into this a bit further, I found that 7.4% of those expenditures are on groceries, which means that the other 5.4% is spent dining out. As you've learned (Day 16), there are multiple ways to save money at the grocery store, just as there are multiple ways to cut back while dining out (Day 17).

These averages help explain why so many Americans struggle to stay ahead of their expenses and to put funds toward paying off debt or planning for the future. But by understanding what Americans' biggest expenses are and by figuring out how you stack up, you can take better stock of your own finances and begin to look for ways to beat those averages. Wouldn't it be nice to have a whole lot more of your income falling under that "Other" category, so that you could be putting a little bit more toward the future every month?

Now that you have completed your first budget, I'd like you to take the time to figure out your personal percentages. How do you stack up against the national averages? Where are you doing well? Where are you struggling? In the spaces on the next page, write your percentages next to the national averages, then offer your thoughts on how you can improve those areas where you fall short in the "notes" column. Is your "Food" percentage high? If so, why? Are you spending more on "Transportation" than you expected? Is your "Medical" percentage low enough to let you think about allocating additional funds to savings? By assessing your averages and how they break down, you can begin to look for new ways to take charge of your finances.

Purchase Category	National Average	My Average	Notes
Food	12.8%		
Clothing	3.6%		
Housing	33.9%		
Entertainment	5.6%		
Medical	5.9%		
Transportation	17%		
Other	21.2%		
Total	100%	100%	

Day 27

The Mechanics of a Monthly Budget Meeting

Over the last few days, you've learned many of the nuances of creating and maintaining a monthly budget. With surprise expenses, surpluses, shortages, price targets and the creation of the budget itself, a lot of energy goes into budgeting. And that should speak volumes about its level of importance. The monthly budget meeting should reinforce this.

A monthly budget meeting is a time to sit down with your significant other (or other person who is directly affected by your spending habits) and evaluate your financial decisions from the previous month and project upcoming budgetary adjustments/consideration.

On Day 22, we talked about three concepts that go hand in hand with budgeting: awareness, communication and accountability. Nowhere are these three concepts more apparent than in your monthly budget meeting. Let's take just a moment to look at how each comes into play, shall we?

Awareness: You're no doubt familiar with my feelings about the positive effects of awareness on your financial decisions. When you pace awareness alongside a discussion with someone else about your finances during your monthly budget meetings, you create something I like to call *hyper-awareness*. It's similar to what happens when you take a project you've been working on in private out to the general public. You're not only likely to become self-conscious, but you begin to second-guess yourself and to evaluate your project anew through their eyes. When it comes to the budget meeting, this hyper-awareness is a good thing because it forces you to view your actions from a completely different perspective than you would have otherwise.

Communication: A constructive financial discussion often involves either admitting your own struggles or being on the receiving end of somebody else's admission (or denial) of the same. It's odd to think that people who know each other intimately have trouble talking about money, but because so much weight is placed on financial stability in our culture, it can be a very sensitive topic. I've seen many cases where, in order to avoid addressing a loved one's issues, one partner in a relationship will volunteer him/herself to take control of and try to compensate for the others' finances. This tactic, however, can have very severe, negative and lasting effects on a relationship. Taking responsibility for somebody else's actions can transform existing roles in the relationship, thereby changing the dynamic of the relationship as a whole. What might seem like a kind and loving gesture can ultimately be the cause of real resentment for all involved.

From the moment you begin sharing financial responsibility with someone, you must open the lines of communication and work together to solve any existing issues. A planned budget meeting between you and your partner is an ideal way of preventing a "spontaneous money conversation." (In other words, a fight.)

Accountability: Examining your spending every month with the person who is affected by your decisions is a surefire way to increase your level of accountability for your actions. If you're in a partnership, both people will be under the same amount of pressure, which is a good thing because, as I noted earlier, it's not enough for one half of a couple to be accountable while the other half passively stands by. You'll quickly figure out which decisions advance your goals and which ones are only hindering your ultimate financial aspirations.

In summary, awareness, communication and accountability are all key components of what should become a regular ritual for anyone who shares financial responsibilities with someone else.

This brings us to the point of today:
Planning your first monthly budget meeting.

The Meeting: Your monthly budget meeting will have three participants: you, your significant other and your budget. It should take place within the first ten days of the month, and the topic should be your spending in the *previous* month. In order to assess your spending, you'll need your detailed checking account statements and credit card statements (both of which you can print out using your bank's online banking system), and any other spending activity statements from that month.

One person will be responsible for reading aloud each transaction, line by line, while the other will be responsible for recording each item in the appropriate category of your budget. Your budget can be managed with simple budgeting software, a basic spreadsheet or even on paper.

As you read through these statements together, each of you will no doubt need to justify a number of your purchases and scrutinize those that don't contribute to your financial goals. You may cringe at the thought of openly airing your finances with your partner, but you need to bite the bullet. Only by honestly discussing your spending habits alongside your financial goals can you make honest assessments and begin to eliminate unnecessary or excessive spending.

Things to look for:

- Overspending
- Bills you forgot to pay
- Loans that you finished paying in the previous month
- Places where you might be able to reduce your monthly spending beyond the 10% you trimmed on Day 25
- Budget projections that were far off track (whether positive or negative)
- Strange spending patterns. For instance, do you go to the same place every Wednesday without realizing it?
- Discrepancies you can dispute with your bank
- Proper credit for merchandise you returned

Things to adjust:

- Price targets
- New expenses you need to add
- Items that have been paid off and thus need to be removed
- Savings deposits that are affected by money you've freed up after paying off a loan or other debt
- Surprise bills that you didn't add previously

Your budget is not a static entity. It will likely change at least a little bit each month, ideally to account for improvements.

This process will lead to tough conversations, but trust me, tough conversations are better than avoiding the topic all together. You are both taking responsibility for your finances, and this is how you begin to make progress. The good news is that ultimately your monthly meetings will get a lot easier.

Day 28

Identify Your Financial Weakness and Put Budget Week Into Perspective

Week Four has probably been one of your toughest weeks yet. Since your budget is the key to getting your financial life in order, it takes time and effort to create and understand. Just remember that some of the most rewarding experiences in life are also the most challenging: graduating from college, running a marathon, starting a business, writing a book, climbing a daunting mountain, being a parent and managing your finances, to name a few.

Budgeting, as you have learned, is about staying organized and taking the time to think and talk through your financial life. It's essential that you not just grasp your monthly budget, but that you get a comprehensive picture of your financial year and are able to make logical budgeting predictions based on the trends and recurring patterns you identify. Get out your calendar. Are there certain periods of the year when you spend large amounts of money? Do you find that you consistently overspend in a particular month? (The family vacation in July? Back-to-school expenses in September? Black Friday shopping in November?) Anticipate and account for these periods of heavy spending in your budget. But as you might have already imagined, sometimes anticipating and accounting for heavy spending just isn't enough. It's very possible that your budget doesn't yet allow you to buy even the simplest of luxuries or entertain the possibility of a month swollen with seasonal purchases. So don't. Not yet, anyway. For now, dedicate yourself to paying off debt, reducing your monthly spending by making more informed buying decisions and slowly freeing up rows on your budget occupied by loans and other non-fixed expenses.

Identify your financial weakness.
In taking a closer look at your budget, you'll no doubt notice one or two pesky items or categories that you constantly struggle with. No matter how hard you try, you just can't seem to commit to reducing your spending in these areas. Many times these budgeting weaknesses show up in areas representing entertainment or vices—rewards for your hard work. Because these things often aren't necessities and don't *require* a budget (although for sake of your sanity, you could easily make an argument to the contrary), the only way to conquer them is to commit to reducing your spending on them. Or in more pronounced cases, sometimes the only way to cut spending is to go cold turkey. Just like any other weakness, logic alone doesn't always provide the ammunition necessary to make the right decisions.

As you are reading this, are you thinking about that item (or several items) in your budget on which you consistently spend beyond your price target? If so, you've just identified your financial weakness(es).

Admit the problem.
Actually, I hate to use the word "problem" here because it suggests there's something wrong with you, when really overspending can be very temporary and common place. So let me rephrase: Admit that you sometimes get off budget. Better yet, admit your financial weakness.

My financial weakness(es):*

_____

_____

_____

*I realize you might feel silly jotting these down in a book—just as with many of the other exercises—but as you might already know, the simple act of admitting that you have a financial weakness (or any weakness, for that matter) is a step that you have to take for lasting change to take place. If you never admit it to yourself, you'll likely never address it, and that's a whole lot sillier than writing it in a book if you ask me. Get to it!

Get budgeting perspective.

If you put the kind of measured financial planning we discussed this week into action, there's simply no way you'll ever have to account for the more obvious budget surprises again. Take the time (as you did on Day 23) to think about the payments you make quarterly, semi-annually and annually. Make sure you put these items in your budget. Vacations, insurance and holidays shouldn't sneak up on you or your budget.

One of the primary goals of budgeting is to determine whether you have a surplus or a shortage each month (Day 24). Are you going deeper into a hole every month? You need to figure this out during your monthly budget meetings (Day 27). It's okay to have a bad month once in a while, but you must be sure you adjust so that the subsequent month is better or even compensates for the shortfall. Simply ignoring the problems caused by a bad month won't make them go away. Address these challenges head on— most often, if you immediately address your financial issues, you will only need to make moderate adjustments to get back on track. But if you wait, ignore or let things fester, you're more likely to face real financial hardship.

The concept of developing price targets (Day 25) within your budget requires some math skills, and fortunately calculators exist. Developing price targets constantly pushes you to be a better spender. Take your three-month spending average per item, and reduce the amount by 10%. Then try to stay under this price target. Knowing your price targets is especially effective for groceries, dining, clothing and entertainment— things that can fluctuate to account for life's necessities.

How did you stack up compared to the National Spending Averages presented on Day 26? The most important takeaway from this information is how crucial it is to have your housing expenses in line. As I've mentioned many times already, overspending on housing is what got many people into a housing mess near the end of 2008. Also, take note of ways to decrease spending in areas like transportation, food and entertainment.

Most importantly, you want to learn from your budgeting experiences and from those of your significant other or the person with whom you share financial responsibility. On Day 27, we covered the mechanics of a monthly budget meeting and discussed the things you should be looking for and adjusting each month. Of course, it's one thing to talk about these things hypothetically, but by actually doing them, you will see what an incredible difference this time will make each month.

Allow the data you gathered from the previous months to teach you how to spend money in the current one. Don't keep banging your head against a wall when it comes to financial weaknesses. If you are overspending adjust. You have all the tools you need to do exactly that right here in this book.

Really.

Next up is risk management. Now that you've learned how to eliminate self-inflicted financial struggle, your understanding of how to manage (and plan for) external, hard-to-predict risks will help you address those things you can't control.

Week Five

Risk Management

Corporations deal with risk management on a regular basis. They project risk, they map out strategies to deal with it and they take precautions to protect themselves from it should it sneak up on them despite their better efforts to ward it off. If you've ever seen a corporate contract, you might have noticed a clause citing protection from "Acts of God." In other words, corporations even take steps to protect themselves from things they can't predict or control.

Individuals, on the other hand, tend to ignore risk unless it comes in the form of a clear and present danger. Sure sometimes risk is intentional. You've probably even heard the saying "the higher the risk, they higher the reward." This refers to another type of risk, though—the strategic kind that people intentionally take in order to transform their conviction or hunches into monetary gain. In Week Five, we're going to talk about the unintentional kind of personal risk—unexpected occurrences that everyone is subject to by virtue of, well, being human. And you're going to learn how to identify, anticipate and take the proper steps to mitigate these unintentional risks before they have the chance to negatively affect your financial life.

Day 29

Come Face-to-Face with Your Risk

You are now 29 days into the 60-day journey, and my hope is that you can already see a brighter financial future. By this point you have built a diverse set of financial skills and strategies, and you have probably figured out that money has less to do with stacks of $50 bills than you once thought. Money, it turns out, is all about discipline and habits, which is why it's entirely possible for someone who makes $40,000/year to be more financially successful than someone who makes $100,000/year.

The kind of disciplined approach you've developed over the previous 28 days *will* pay off in the end. But no matter how disciplined you are, life can strike at any time and alter even the most carefully-thought-out plans. I'm not trying to rain on your parade here, but, hey, sometimes rain happens. The magic is in the backup plan.

Do you see where I'm going with this? Yep, I'm planning for the worst. Because of the curve balls life can throw you, it's important to make sure that no matter what happens, you—and your family—can still achieve your financial goals. Emergency and contingency planning are vital for this reason. Your financial life has to account for the possibility of huge unexpected risks like losing your job, wrecking your car or becoming seriously ill, to name a few. Unlike the surprise expenses we talked about on Day 23, these expenses usually can't be predicted, which is unfortunate considering they have the potential to create long-lasting financial disaster. The good news, though, is that because everyone is subject to these things, there are several ways to prepare for and protect yourself from them.

"Planning for risk is not pessimistic; it's smart."

Which brings up an important point: because these things are unpleasant to think about, we often don't. But we need to.

Come face-to-face with risk.
Our task today is for you to develop an understanding of which risks would most hurt you, your family and your financial situation, and how prepared you currently are to cope with them.

1. **Identify the risks that exist in your life.** In the following table, I've listed some of the more common risks that people face. But everybody's situation is different, so you can likely add specific risks based on your knowledge of family illnesses, investments or other pending issues that are unique to you and your family's situation.

2. **Rank your level of exposure to each risk.** On a scale of 1 to 3, on which "1" indicates the highest level of financial preparedness and "3" indicates the lowest, rate your level of exposure to these risks.

> **NOTE:** This may prove to be a difficult assignment if you don't know what constitutes being adequately prepared for risk. If this is the case, rank your level of preparation relative to that of other items on this list, and then revisit and re-rank each item at the end of this week when you are better qualified to assess your exposure to risk.

---

3. **Rate each risk's relative impact on your family.** Ask yourself to what extent your financial life and that of your family would be affected by the following emergencies. Using a scale similar to the one presented in the last step, rate each risk based on priority—"1" being the highest priority (or having the highest impact) and "3" being the lowest.

4. **Identify your most urgent risks.** Clearly those items with the potential for the highest level of impact on you and your family are those for which you should be the most prepared. As you go through these potential risks, take special note of any that you rate as having a high impact but a low level of preparedness. These are going to be the most urgent ones for you to address this week. In the far right column, rate high-urgency items as "1," medium-urgency items as "2" and low-urgency items as "3."

The Risk, Preparation, Impact and Urgency Table

Risk	Preparation (1-3)	Impact (1-3)	Urgency (1-3)
Death			
Disability			
Job loss			
Extended illness			

Car accident			
Loss due to bad investments or stock-market crash			
My/my family's unique risk:			
My/my family's unique risk:			
My/my family's unique risk:			

While it's obviously impossible to prevent things like death or disability, the point of this worksheet is to determine whether you are prepared for them financially—or whether you need to start preparing now.

If, as you thought through each of these items, you wondered how one might prepare for one or more of them, it likely means that you haven't done so. For now, just put a "3" in the right column next to each item that stumped you to indicate your low level of preparedness here. We'll talk about exactly *how* to prepare for these things over the next six days.

Just because you can't eliminate risks entirely, it doesn't mean you can't reduce their power to cause damage to your financial life.

Day 30

Identify True Financial Emergencies

In order to deal with a financial emergency correctly, you have to be able to identify it accurately. It's not uncommon for people to mistake difficult financial times for real financial crises and, in the process, deplete whatever emergency funds they have to resolve them. Thus, one of the first things you must learn to do is distinguish a true financial emergency from a mere financial alarm. While both situations require a fast response, learning to differentiate them will allow you to respond appropriately, using the optimum tools from your financial arsenal.

The good news is that distinguishing between financial emergencies and those that only *seem* like emergencies is a skill you can master quickly. The trick is to first familiarize yourself with the types of solutions that exist to resolve each type of problem, as these will allow you to gauge a proper response. Then you must understand which challenges can be anticipated (non-emergencies) and which cannot (emergencies).

The tool you use to remedy a financial snafu will generally fall into one of two basic categories:

Pre-funded solutions. These tools are monetary precautions you've taken as a result of reviewing your budget closely and predicting upcoming shortfalls. Pre-funded solutions will help you offset foreseeable problems that have a high probability of occurrence.

Emergency solutions. These tools are the result of regularly putting money into emergency funds and other savings accounts, properly insuring yourself and of setting up a will for dependents. Emergency solutions will help you offset financial crises and truly unforeseeable emergencies.

When assessing a financial obstacle, ask yourself, "Which one of these solutions will it require?" Seems pretty easy, right? That's because it is. But knowing the solutions is only one half of the challenge.

You must also take the proper steps to ensure you are using the *correct* solution. If a problem requires only a pre-funded solution but is solved with an emergency one, we open ourselves to real vulnerability in a true financial crisis.

All too often, a lack of preparedness for non-emergency expenses creates major problems because it forces you to deplete your emergency funds or go into debt. Debt is clearly not the appropriate solution—often not even in the case of emergencies. The key is to prepare yourself for foreseeable expenses before they happen and to build an emergency reserve for those truly unexpected crises. If going into debt is your current backup plan, it's time to change that. All of the tools you need to establish your artillery of pre-funded solutions are provided in the first half of this book, and we'll work on building a repertoire of emergency ones in the second half.

The bottom line is that you need to be able to distinguish between an emergency and a non-emergency and to have the correct solutions at your disposal should either occur.

Emergencies	Non-Emergencies
• A car accident	• Forgetting to pay a bill
• Job loss	• Accruing multiple
• An accident on	overdraft fees
your property	• Spontaneous major
• Chronic health issues	purchase
or disease	• Overspending of any kind
• Medical issues that	• Holiday shopping
do not fall under regular	• Clearance sale
preventive care	• Gambling
• A robbery	• Buying a car
• Home foreclosure or other	
asset seizure	
• Any legal matters	

One thing I should mention is that an emergency is not always life threatening. Consider this situation: your child throws a football through your church's two-hundred-year-old stained glass window. You will need to pay for the window, but there was no way for you to anticipate this expense. This is an emergency. On the other hand, forgetting about your commitment to the church's annual fund-raising campaign until the night before pledges are due does not qualify as emergency because it was a foreseeable expense and does not require, under any circumstances, an emergency solution.

The most important thing to remember? Just because you aren't financially prepared for an event doesn't make it a financial emergency. In short, the ability to plan—and anticipate—is the key factor that distinguishes a non-emergency from an emergency.

Emergency? Or Non-Emergency?

Below are some common financial hurdles. All of the situations involve immediate demands for money, but are they emergencies? It's time to test your judgment. Which ones are true financial emergencies that require turning to your emergency fund? And which should be solved through financial shuffling and discipline? Circle one for each question.

1. You get a bill in the mail for your license plates. You forgot about them and you owe $200.

   Emergency   Non-emergency

2. Your anniversary is next week. You want to buy your wife a pair of diamond earrings, but you haven't saved any money to do so.

   Emergency   Non-emergency

3. You rear-end someone while sending text messages and have to pay the $500 deductible on your car insurance.

   Emergency   Non-emergency

4. Your dog inhales a candy bar, and you have to take him to the vet as a result.

   Emergency   Non-emergency

5. Your best friends take a spontaneous trip to Chicago for the weekend, and they want you to come and share in all the fun.

   Emergency   Non-emergency

6. Your children will not shut up about the new Xbox 360.
    The only way to get them to leave you alone is to buy them one.

    Emergency   Non-emergency

7. You have a near-death experience while choking on a French fry,
    and (after a friend administers the Heimlich maneuver) you decide
    to buy term life insurance. The premium is $500 for the year.

    Emergency   Non-emergency

8. You find your favorite wine on sale by the case. You want to buy
    two cases, which will put a serious dent in your wallet, but they
    will last you at least two years, which will save you money in the
    long term.

    Emergency   Non-emergency

9. It's mid-January, and you are sick of shoveling snow. You want to
    buy a snow blower.

    Emergency   Non-emergency

10. Your college roommate calls you to borrow money. He just needs
    $1,000 to get him through a tough time.

    Emergency   Non-emergency

To some people these questions will seem insultingly obvious. But I know
from experience that many people will also really struggle to answer
them, which is why I've gone to such lengths to help distinguish between
emergencies and financial challenge.

You cannot depend on your savings, emergency funds or other long-term financial precautions when life throws you a curve ball and you've failed to plan. Emergency funds are for emergencies. Going over budget—or into debt—is a financial decision that should be considered only in times of true crisis. So take the time to learn the difference between the things you can predict and those you can't and plan accordingly. That way you can avoid or prevent any need to consider tapping into your reserves for unnecessary or foreseeable expenses. Otherwise, you'll deplete your emergency funds and find yourself unprepared for real financial emergencies.

Key: 1. Non-emergency 2. Non-emergency 3. Emergency 4. Emergency 5. Non-emergency

6. Non-emergency 7. Non-emergency 8. Non-emergency 9. Non-emergency 10. Non-emergency

Day 31

Build Your Emergency Fund

As we go through Week Five, you will notice just how many precautions you can take to offset unforeseeable events that result in financial emergency. Different types of insurance protect you in case of disability, accidents, fires, robbery, health emergencies, you name it. Wills and trusts protect your dependents in the case of your untimely death, and various precautions exist to protect you from identity theft. But what about those things that aren't covered by insurance or other such precautionary tools? What about that broken church window from Day 30? Or monetary loss from a bad investment? Or a job loss?

There are many truly random and unpredictable risks for which there is no external remedy. Many would argue that this is what credit cards are for, but assuming you've read the pages leading up to this chapter, you know that credit absolutely should not be your go-to solution for emergencies. Instead, you should become self-sufficient in the face of emergencies by building an emergency fund to offset unexpected risks.

It can take years to build up an emergency reserve that fully protects you, but many of life's random risks do not require a lifetime's worth of emergency funds. What you're looking for is enough money to cover you and your family, should an unexpected problem render your income obsolete for a short period of time.

In Week One, you determined your goals as they relate to emergency funds. This week we are discussing their direct applications and importance, and in Week Seven, we'll talk extensively about savings as a whole. Today, we're going to cover the basics of creating an emergency fund. Your ultimate goal is to build an emergency fund that will allow you to cover three months' worth of expenses, should one of life's unexpected events render you unable to generate income during that time. This may take you several years to accomplish, but in light of all the risks out there, it is definitely worth the time and effort.

Calculate your target emergency fund.
What are your total monthly expenses? $_____
Multiply that amount by 3 (months) $_____
This is your target emergency fund.

Determine how much you need to save to create this fund.
How much do you have in your savings account right now? $_____

Subtract this number from your target emergency fund
(as established above): $_____

This is how much you need to save to create your emergency fund.

If you already have your target emergency funds reserved, you will learn specifically what to do with them in Week Seven. If you have a shortage, you will need to put a portion of your net monthly income into your emergency reserve each month as part of your overall savings strategy, which we will also discuss in Week Seven.

For now, just keep this number in mind as a reminder that sometimes you have to come up with financial solutions to problems you had no part in creating.

Day 32

Find an Insurance Agent

Insurance is vital when it comes to managing risk for you, your family and your finances, which means it's crucial that you trust the people involved in your dealings in this area. Yet insurance is one category in which people (younger people, especially) tend to ignore the importance and value of trusted relationships.

Insurance companies exacerbate this impersonal approach. Their marketing campaigns encourage consumers to see pricing as the primary value differentiator and to make purchasing minimum coverage from anonymous agents via a toll-free number seem normal. You deserve better than anonymous, one-size-fits-all advice. And do you really want to navigate the complexities of insurance without a trusted guide?

Insurance is tricky. You want to have great insurance, but you never want to have to use it. And the moment you use it, your premiums go up and you find yourself with fewer good coverage options. Why? Because your ability to obtain most types of insurance is based on your claims history. (A claim, of course, is when you "use" your insurance. You are claiming your right to compensation under the terms of the policy.) The more often you make these claims, the bigger the risk you present to the insurer. A greater number of claims makes a company more likely to increase your premium costs and less likely to insure you.

And that's where most people's knowledge of insurance ends.

Because of this, you can benefit from talking to an expert about your insurance coverage. For example, nearly every state requires you to buy car insurance and maintain minimum coverage levels on it. Why not buy it from an agent who can explain how to combine your auto insurance policy with other policies? It may cost a few dollars more, but an agent who understands your situation fully can find you the best options for protecting *all* of your assets. People tend to forget that insurance isn't just about replacing or repairing damaged cars or houses. It's about protecting yourself in the case of an emergency ("emergency" is again defined as any unforeseeable event that results in severe financial consequences). As you have probably gathered by now, there are a number of types of emergencies that can blindside you at any time.

What else can you learn from a trusted insurance agent that you won't learn from a faceless customer service representative at a call center?

1. **There are several different types of insurance out there—some of which make sense for you and others that don't.** Insurance, for example, will protect your financial assets if you are sued as a result of an accident. (This is liability coverage.) If you think this isn't likely to happen to you, consider this scenario: someone slips and falls on your property and sues you as a result. Not only is this well within their rights, but many times they win. If you don't have the right liability coverage, the court can and will go after your assets.

Or consider the complexities of a home fire. You need to make sure that you have the proper contents coverage so that you will be fully compensated for replacements.

And then there's comprehensive homeowners coverage, something for which I was very thankful when my house was broken into a few years back. The policy allowed me to seek and receive reimbursement for all of the stolen items.

2. **The greater your coverage with one company, the larger the discount they are likely to offer on any or all of the policies you carry with them.**

3. **Different insurance companies place different levels of emphasis on your credit.** If your credit score is subpar, you may be able to save money by switching to a carrier that doesn't weigh credit scores as heavily in determining rates for customers. You might be surprised by how much something as seemingly unrelated to insurance as your credit score can affect your premiums. But it can, and a good insurance agent will take this into consideration when helping you find the best policies.

You might be thinking, "Well, now that you've told me all of this, why should I hire an insurance agent to tell me again?" Let me assure you that in the complex world of insurance, there are far more than three nuances that can drastically affect your insurance coverage and overall success. For the same reason that I haven't listed all of them here, you should find an insurance agent pronto: there are simply way too many details to take into account when it comes to insurance.

Start to get a handle on your current insurance situation by listing the carriers of your different insurance policies in the table provided on the following page.

Type of insurance	Carrier
Homeowners	
Renters	
Auto	
Life	
Health	
Disability	
Contents	

Based on this table, you should now have a better sense of your insurance "big picture." Next, if you can answer "yes" to one or more of the following questions, you should consider restructuring your current insurance situation and engaging an insurance agent as part of that process.

- Do you have multiple insurance carriers?
- Have you taken a piecemeal approach to coverage, sometimes hopping around for the best rate, going with friends' recommendations or with your historic provider, or assuming that rates were pretty much the same?
- Are you *not* insured for something you should be?
- Are you unsure what your insurance will actually cover?
- Is the only direct contact you've ever had with an insurance company a nameless representative through the company's 800 number?
- Do you have more than one insurance agent?

If you are motivated to change your current insurance situation, you should have three goals:

1. **Find a trusted insurance agent.**
   Just as with finding a trusted financial advisor, I recommend you find a trusted insurance agent by asking your friends and family for recommendations. You want to find someone with a proven track record to help you effectively manage the risk in your life. A good agent will ask you many questions that are meant to determine if your risks are properly mitigated. You should talk to your insurance agent at least once a year to update him/her on the developments in your life.

2. **Work to secure a multi-policy discount.**
   This doesn't mean you should buy a policy you don't need; it means that you should trim the fat wherever possible by having one company cover you for the different types of coverage you need.

That said, I have two caveats: 1) Sometimes it is more cost effective to take out policies with different companies, and it is worth taking the time to find out. 2) Sometimes the agent you trust to advise you and ensure that you have the right coverage will not work with the company that offers you the best deal. In this case, it may be worth it to pay a little extra for peace of mind.

3. **Make sure you have the proper insurance.**
   The prospect of getting sued because your dog bites someone, the chance of a house fire claiming all of your possessions or the possibility of losing your great-grandmother's jewelry in a burglary is each reason enough to find a good insurance agent who understands your insurance portfolio.

Day 33

Buy Life Insurance

I don't quite know how to cushion this blow, so I'm just going to say it: you are going to die. Sorry. It's true. And if you haven't come to terms with this reality, then you likely haven't addressed its effects either. Nothing will destroy your family's financial future quicker than your premature death. But you can minimize the damage to their finances by taking the proper steps to insure your life.

Generally speaking, there is no less comfortable topic to address with a loved one than life insurance. (Some people might even prefer death itself to having a conversation about life insurance.) But comfortable or not, it's important to determine what happens to your assets (and liabilities) in the event of your death. Believe me, I've been there to pick up the pieces for people who decided it was better to avoid an awkward conversation than to plan for a secure future for their loved ones. This truly is a financial disaster, but one that can be easily avoided by treating life insurance as a given in your financial planning and purchasing a policy that will adequately cover your dependents in the case of your untimely death.

There are two primary types of life insurance coverage: term and permanent. Choosing between the two different types of life insurance can be difficult.

Term life insurance

Term life insurance is the least expensive option. If you are struggling financially, term insurance is, without a doubt, the best solution for you. Under a term policy, you buy a block of insurance, known as the "face amount," to cover a set period of time. During this time, you are responsible for an annual premium, which can be paid monthly, quarterly, semi-annually or annually. For example, if you buy $250,000 worth of face amount for 20 years, you can die (sorry, it had to be said!) any time in that 20 years, and your beneficiaries will receive $250,000. After 20 years, the policy expires, and if you die, your beneficiaries do not receive anything.

Permanent life insurance

The first thing you should know about permanent life insurance is that, contrary to what its name suggests, it isn't necessarily permanent. There are two main reasons for this. The first is that if you stop paying the premium, there is a very likely possibility that your coverage will expire. The second— and more complicating—factor is that policies such as universal life and variable universal life are dependent on "cash accounts" that are subject to the vagaries of either interest rates or the stock market. As you age, your premium is calculated based on how much money is in your cash account, and if things work the way they should this money reserve helps keep your premium reasonable. But because your cash account is subject to interest rates, there is also risk: if interest rates go down during the life of the policy, there might not be enough cash to cover the premium cost later in the policy. Thus, the policy dies...before you do. You can prevent this, however, by making sure that your insurance policy has a coverage guarantee, which will ensure your coverage until the day you die. If you already have permanent life insurance, you will want to make sure that you have a coverage guarantee—older policies do not always have this feature.

If you're confused, consider this yet another reason why you should find a trusted insurance agent. It's important that you understand these risks, and that you address them when you buy life insurance. The worst thing you can do is let the complexity of life insurance dissuade you from participating in a policy. In general, if funded properly, these policies will last until the day you die.

Permanent life insurance is more expensive than term insurance, but can be a good financial strategy for those who are on stable financial ground. I do not, however, recommend permanent life insurance if you struggle financially. The good news is that *60 Days to Change* can eliminate the struggle, but for some people the path to financial stability and good habits will take months if not years. If you are bogged down by debt, lack emergency reserves and are still trying to develop strong financial habits, don't burden yourself with another overwhelming expense—stick with term life insurance.

The most important thing to know about life insurance is that you should buy the proper amount regardless of whether you purchase permanent or term coverage. If you need $500,000 worth of life insurance (a very common and reasonable amount), but can only afford $100,000 worth of permanent, buy term coverage. I cannot emphasize this point enough. Really. If I could show up in your living room and shake you by the shoulders, I would. Do you hear me?? Buy the proper amount!

Which brings us to this question:

How much life insurance do you need?

Being overinsured or underinsured are both unfavorable situations, but the potential consequences of being underinsured are far worse. Now that you are aware of your need to adequately insure yourself, neglecting this responsibility is unacceptable. Take this from a guy who has cleaned up the financial messes of those who died uninsured or underinsured.

As an absolute baseline, you need enough life insurance to pay off your debts to the world (or at least your creditors). But being *properly* insured requires a slightly more complicated formula. First and foremost, you must declare your intentions. Are you trying to leave an income stream for your loved ones? Are you trying to leave a legacy for generations to come? Or are you simply trying to cover your final expenses? Each of these intentions will produce a different insurance need; for now, however, I'm going to focus on the first one, creating an income stream for your loved ones. It is economically efficient, and it is the most common use of life insurance.

If you didn't have life insurance and you died today, your income would die with you. Your dependents would suffer as a result. (I told you this was an uncomfortable topic.) How can you replace income that disappears when you do? By buying life insurance. Let's say that you make $50,000 per year. Your net income is somewhere in the range of $35,000 per year (after taxes, benefits, and other deductions). Do you know how much life insurance it would take to replace a net income of $35,000 per year indefinitely? About $700,000.[1] I'll pause for a moment while you recover from that number. Okay, yes, that's a lot of insurance. But the reality is, if you are trying to provide your income to your family for the rest of their lives, you are going to need this amount of life insurance.

Let me interject with a quick explanation for those of you who are reading this and wondering, "Why do I need to provide for my family for the rest of their lives? I'll support my kids until they're 18 but after that, they can get a job!" Generally speaking, your primary concern should be to support your spouse and any dependents who are unable to provide for themselves.

---

[1] What's the math on this? It is safe to assume that your dependents would be provided an indefinite stream of income of $35,000/year based on the assumption that a diversified portfolio funded by the $700,000 death benefit would be able to produce a 5% rate of return. This return would be your income. As long as you live off the rate-of-return income ($35,000), then the principal ($700,000) would never deplete.

Of course, people have many objectives for their life insurance. Supporting their dependents—whether capable of working or not—is often one of them. For the purposes of this book, life insurance is suggested in the case of the premature death of someone with dependents or a spouse. You have the right to decide how long you want to provide income to your spouse in the event of your death. I personally have planned to provide my family with lifetime income in the event of my untimely death. This is a personal decision that you have to make, but my two cents are that you should provide them income for the rest of their lives.

There is the possibility that you may not need a great deal of life insurance, specifically if you are single, independently wealthy or don't have children. Your situation, however, could change unexpectedly as an effect of one of the risks we're focusing on this week, and because of that, you should make sure that you try to secure coverage when you are young and healthy. Trying to buy an extensive amount of coverage when you're in your late forties or fifties can be cost prohibitive.

Determine how much life insurance you will need in order to secure your current lifestyle for your family by answering the following:

What is your net (after taxes and deductions) income?
$ _____

Divide your net income by .05. (I'll wait while you grab a calculator.)
$ _____

The number you just calculated is the amount of life insurance that it would take to reproduce your income indefinitely for dependents covered by your policy. More specifically, this number is based on an income derived by a 5% rate of return on the principal of a diversified portfolio (a group of investments including stocks, bonds and/or mutual funds).

Don't get all hot and bothered by the mechanics of life insurance, though. To put it in perspective, it costs about $25 per month for $500,000 worth of term insurance for a 30-year-old. That is not a tremendous amount of money to spend on adequately protecting your family.

Know that if you think you can beat the system and skimp on coverage, you're wrong. Why do that to your family? Sometimes it is as easy as foregoing one meal out per month to easily afford the appropriate amount of life insurance.

One additional note: you may be tempted to obtain your life insurance through your benefits package at work. I urge you to reconsider that idea. Most group life insurance plans are not portable. This means that you can't take the coverage with you if you separate (voluntarily or involuntarily) from your job. At least 75% of the total coverage that you need should be purchased outside of work. This simple little formula will prevent you from exposing your family to risks should you lose your job.

Are you adequately protected?
Answer the following questions to assess your situation.

- How much life insurance do you have outside of work?

- How much life insurance do you have through work?

- What percentage of your overall coverage does this represent?

- Does your total amount of life insurance equal the "coverage needed" amount you calculated earlier today?

- If not, how much life insurance do you need to acquire?

Life insurance isn't fun or flashy, but it will help replace your income in the event of your death—and that can make the difference between a life of stability and one in the poorhouse (or the modern-day equivalent) for your loved ones. And remember, life insurance is far less expensive when the insured is young and healthy. Don't wait too long to buy the coverage you need. You can purchase life insurance from your insurance agent, financial advisor or online. But as always, I recommend that you do it through a professional. There is no time quite like the present to do it.

Don't make me come over to your house and shake you...

Day 34

Develop a Will or Trust

The importance of having "final documents" goes far beyond conventional or traditional wisdom, which for years suggested that only the wealthy needed a will or trust. This is simply not the case. Everyone needs final documents of some sort. The more complicated your life and your financial affairs, the more complex the documents you will need. If you have a particular area of your life that you would like sorted out after your death, you need to prepare the legal documents to allow for it. Whether you are a 35-year-old single parent with one child, a pre-retiree in your late fifties with few health problems or a young parent of a special needs child, you need to consider the legal ramifications of your death or disability.

In the paragraphs that follow, I lay out the key aspects of estate planning.

Disclaimer: I am not an attorney. You would be able to tell this if you were at a cocktail party with me, but since you're not, I feel obligated to make that clear. This section is not to be construed as legal advice. It is merely a discussion of different legal tools that will help mitigate financial risk. For specific legal advice, consult an attorney licensed in your state.

What is a will?

A will is a legal document that states your intentions for your estate after your death. These intentions include the distribution of your assets and property. A will may also dictate how other business and personal affairs will be handled after your death.

What is a trust?

A trust is a legal document that holds property or assets for the benefit of a beneficiary and is managed by a trustee. There are many types of trusts such as: A/B Trusts, Irrevocable Trusts, Living Trusts and Testamentary Trusts. Your need for these (and other) types of trusts is completely dependent on your specific financial and legal situation.

How does a will or trust fit into the risk management strategy I'm working on in Week Five?

A will or trust is all about offsetting financial emergencies for your family. Sure, if you were to die without a will your finances would still go to your immediate family, but not leaving them with detailed instructions can lead to a world of hurt. The purpose of a will or trust is to save your family from difficult (and often biased) decisions in your absence. By taking the time to prepare appropriate legal documents now, you are making your wishes known so that nobody has to guess in the case of your death or a disability that prevents you from effectively communicating your wishes.

How to get started.

You will not be able to determine whether you need a will and/or trust by reading this section. You will, however, be able to answer some very important questions that will help you better prepare for any future legal dealings on the subject. Your attention to these questions is paramount to your family's financial security. Take the time to consider each question thoroughly, and be sure to discuss your answers with your partner or spouse.

- Who will receive your assets and property in the event of your death?
- Who will take care of your children if you die while they are still under your care?
- Who will take care of your assets and property for the benefit of your children in the event of your death?
- Who is authorized to make end-of-life decisions for you?
- Who is authorized to make medical decisions for you if you become incapacitated?

As I mentioned, not addressing these questions prior to your death sets a dangerous precedent. Your family and friends, who will be grieving, will be forced to make difficult decisions. Don't assume that your family will naturally figure out the best steps to take: do it for them. Doing so will prevent unnecessary heartache and headaches for them. And to top it all off, having legal documents will prevent your family and friends from disagreeing on your intentions. You'd be surprised how quickly this can escalate. Just imagine your mother pitted against your mother-in-law. I've seen it happen and it's not pretty. Do not put them in this position.

Some legal experts believe that you can accomplish a basic level of protection by completing legal documents online. There are a number of online tools that help you prepare legal documents according to the laws of the state in which you reside. You can find many options by going to your favorite search engine and searching the phrase "will and trust."

Ultimately, it's in your family's best interest for you to investigate your legal options for a will or trust, and you should do this without delay. Once you have had a chance to think about and answer the five questions above, you can begin to take the steps that are most appropriate for you.

Day 35

Avoid Identity Theft

When it comes to managing risk, there's no way to avoid a conversation about identity theft. Identity theft is one of the most common crimes and can instantaneously destroy the financial life you've carefully built over the years.

It may seem like a moderate inconvenience, but identity theft is a major event that can take months or years to clear up. I should know—I was a victim of identity theft back in 1998. I left my wallet and checkbook in my car (yes, I know, it was a genius move on my part), and sure enough, my car was broken into. The thief was able to open a credit card at a local store, and also wrote numerous checks from my checking account. Dealing with this fraudulent activity consumed my life for four months. I don't know what was more painful—dealing with the ramifications of identity theft or nursing my wounded pride after being so careless. To think I wasted four months of my life tending to a problem that I could have so easily avoided.

Capitalizing on people's fears of identity theft, several "identity protection" services have popped up in recent years. Some are stand-alone companies, and some are divisions or subsidiaries of credit card and insurance companies. It is not absolutely necessary to purchase identity theft coverage, but in my experience it is reasonable. The following are a few steps you can take on your own before you drop up to $120/year on identity protection.

At a minimum, make sure you adopt these protective strategies:

1. **Don't carry your life in your wallet or purse.** Leave your Social Security card and your birth certificate in a safe-deposit box or in a safe place at home. You don't need them on a daily basis. It's not uncommon to misplace your wallet, and there's really no reason to give thieves a head start.

2. **Be careful when opening unsolicited emails.** One of the most common causes of identity theft is email "phishing" scams. As a precaution, never click on links in email messages that allegedly come from your financial institutions, cell-phone provider or utility companies. Many of these links take you to websites that look frighteningly similar to the corporate ones they're imitating, but really they're just attempts to steal your login information. Always go directly to the website by typing in the known web address, not the one in your email.

3. **Shred *everything*.** Never place a single account statement in the trash without first shredding it. Not only that—don't put your garbage out until collection day. This may sound overly cautious, but investing in a shredder and taking these simple steps are minor adjustments that can prevent a major headache.

4. **Don't choose lame usernames and passwords.** There are many areas in my life where my primary goal is simply to not be lame (something I'm sure will become more challenging as my daughter gets older and I inevitably become lamer), but when it comes to identity theft I have to go above and beyond "not lame" and become downright creative. Creativity is critical when it comes to the usernames and passwords used to access any account associated with your identity or your money. One very uncreative tactic to avoid? Using any combination of your name and/or birth

date in your passwords. Because so many people do this, it's one of the first things a hacker will try when attempting to get into your account(s). Trust me, there are not many combinations you can create from these two pieces of information.

Many sites are now taking matters into their own hands by requiring users to combine a series of numbers, punctuation marks, symbols and uppercase and lowercase letters when creating passwords.

Also, don't store your passwords on your computer—if someone hacks into or steals your computer, you don't want them to have easy access to all of your sensitive information. Instead, keep a list of your usernames and passwords in a safe place near your desk if you can't remember them all.

5. **Check your credit report every year.** Previously, we discussed the importance of checking your credit report every year to track your financial standing, and this time around you should do it for your identity's sake. It would be unfortunate to find out that your identity was stolen five years ago, and that another you is alive and well, living in Boca Raton and wreaking havoc on your good financial name. Stay on top of your credit report by monitoring it on a regular basis. (Unlike a formal request for a credit report by a utility company or landlord, checking your credit on your own, through a site like AnnualCreditReport.com, will not affect your credit.)

You have worked too hard at building a strong financial life simply to have some unsavory character screw up your progress. Don't take the safety of your identity for granted. Completing the items on this checklist will give you peace of mind and protect your assets.

Recovering from identity theft

If, by chance, you are a victim of identity theft, you need to try to recover as quickly as possible. If your identity has been stolen, there is a good chance that your credit has already suffered or will suffer in the future. The quicker you repair your credit, the better.

The Federal Trade Commission (FTC) is so concerned with the prevalence of identity theft that they have defined a very specific set of steps to help you recover from this crime. Here is what you need to do to recover from identity theft:

1. **Place fraud alerts on your credit reports.** Contact the three different credit bureaus (I provided their names and contact information on Day 8), and place fraud alerts to begin the process of making each aware of your concerns. This can prevent the fraud from getting worse.

2. **Close the accounts that have been tampered with.** If an account was opened as a result of the fraud or if fraudulent activity occurred on an account that you already have, close the account. Assuming you have a balance on the account, you will have to transfer the balance to another account (even if the charges aren't yours) while you're going through this process, but at least the person who has assumed your identity won't be able to make any further purchases on the account. Closing the affected account is the surest way to prevent the problem from worsening.

3. **File a complaint with the FTC.** This will allow them to add your case to their extensive research of identity theft, and it will help them prevent future fraud—yours included. The sad truth is that identity theft can happen more than once. You can file your complaint at www. FTC.gov.

4. **File a report with your local police.** There may be particular
    aspects of your identity-theft case that match up with other cases
    in your area. Believe it or not, this could help you find and stop the
    offender—a luxury that many identity theft victims don't have the
    opportunity to enjoy.

Identity theft isn't a petty crime, and its victims often face long-term
financial setbacks as a result. Be vigilant and wary of identity theft, and take
precautions to prevent it.

Week Six

Employee Benefits and Your Career

Because your income is your most important financial resource and your job is usually responsible for the majority of your income, jobs have their own complexities and nuances you must carefully consider. As you're no doubt beginning to see, money—in all of its incarnations—tends to come with strings attached. An oversimplified explanation for this is that there's often a direct correlation between the level of importance we assign to something and the level of difficulty involved in managing it. Considering our income allows us to fund our lifestyles, provide for our families and support our overall financial goals, I think it's safe to say that most Americans have a lot riding on their jobs.

This week we're going to focus on the income, benefits and challenges that result from your job. You must not only understand your job as it exists today; you need to formulate a career backup plan should it *not* exist in the future. If a layoff has already hit you, you'll learn essentials for finding another job.

When it comes to your number-one source of income, there's a lot lying below the surface that you need to consider as you work your way toward financial freedom.

Day 36

Examine Your Employee Benefits

For years, Americans took for granted the fact that their employers provided them with health insurance, life insurance and retirement plans as part of their standard compensation packages. Now, as employers struggle to keep up with the cost of providing benefits to their entire workforces, they're often faced with a difficult decision: eliminate positions or slash employee benefits. Clearly, the latter option is the lesser of these two evils, but it doesn't come without its challenges. It puts many Americans in the unfamiliar position of paying up to half of their monthly health insurance premiums. And because the cost of insurance is projected to continue rising, this is no small burden on the American workforce.

Health care may be the most visible employee benefit, but benefits can include everything from vacation and flex time to company-subsidized lunches and on-site childcare. For the purposes of Day 36, however, we will focus on examining those benefits to which employees contribute, such as insurance, retirement plans and services. Each category is unique, and each requires your understanding. To make sure you fully understand how to get the most from your benefits, let's start by taking inventory of them. What does your employer currently offer, and what benefits are you currently taking advantage of? How much does each cost you every month?

Benefit	Does your company offer it?	Are you taking advantage of it?	Cost per month
Health insurance			
Dental insurance			
Disability insurance			
Group life insurance			
Retirement plan			
Legal services			
Childcare			

Now that you've taken inventory of your benefits, you should know which ones you have access to, what you are taking advantage of (or not) and how much you spend on each item each month. This information is valuable in that it will allow you to accurately assess what changes, if any, you need to make in order to ensure you're adequately covered. You may find that even though you're taking advantage of your employer's health care, the monthly premium is high and the plan doesn't offer you the coverage you need. For example, maybe you need to see a specialist every month, but your plan only covers emergencies. In this case, you might be better off exploring outside options. Or maybe you've been putting off legal services because you didn't think you could afford them, but now you've discovered that your job will supplement the costs. Suddenly things are looking up in the world. I'm telling you, the power of information never ceases to amaze.

Health insurance benefits are typically considered the most important of all, as you are generally better covered—at a lower cost to you—under employer plans. Not only will you pay less, but when you obtain health insurance through your employer, your pre-existing conditions are unlikely to negatively affect your eligibility or premiums. Outside of employment, on the other hand, there are few affordable insurance solutions that won't deny you coverage based on pre-existing conditions—or charge you prohibitively-expensive premiums.

The bottom line is this: you need health insurance. As you learned last week in our discussion of risk management, insurance can prevent an unfortunate event from turning into a financial disaster, so it is imperative that you identify a coverage option.

Day 37

Understand Employer-Sponsored Retirement Plans

An old metaphor in the retirement-planning community compares your retirement income sources to a three-legged stool. (Incidentally, I've heard three different people claim credit for the metaphor, so I won't bother to do the same.) The three legs of the stool represent your employee pension, Social Security benefits and personal retirement savings.

These days, chances are your good ol' three-legged American stool is missing one or two legs. The reality is that if you are younger than 50, you are missing at least one leg of the stool because Social Security is becoming less and less reliable as the years tick on. Other missing legs? Pensions are now about as common as VCRs. And the *coup de grace* is that Americans' retirement assets have dwindled to dangerous lows.

Dan Veto, President of Retirement Spark!, a retirement research and consulting firm, notes:

> "The golden years of government- and employer-provided retirement financial security, if in fact they ever really existed, are over. Individuals must come to terms with this and recognize that they [should] not entrust their financial future to either their employer or their government. Instead, individuals and couples

must feel personally responsible for ensuring their own retirement financial security and take action accordingly."

The harsh reality of 21st-century American retirement shouldn't discourage you from trying to save for the future. (In fact, it should make you even more determined.) But beware, your retirement income will most likely be funded solely by the retirement funds you save on your own. Unless major changes take place in Social Security, you shouldn't count on it as a post-retirement source of income, especially if you were born after 1964.

So where should you start? If your company provides one, participate in a sponsored retirement plan such as a 401(k), 401(a), 403(b) or 457. (These are different from pensions or employer-*funded* retirement plans, which have all but disappeared.) You really don't have a choice as to which plan you can contribute to. Your employer will give you access to a retirement plan based on the type of business entity they are. Hospitals, schools, government offices and private businesses all use different types of plans. But they are basically all the same to you, and the important thing is that you participate. If your employer has a 403(b), participate. If your employer offers a 457 plan, participate. If your employer offers a 401(k), participate.

Your participation, no matter what the plan, is essential to your future financial security, and with structured arrangements through your employer, you can automatically devote a part of every month's paycheck to your retirement without having to think about it. Some employer-sponsored retirement plans even match your payments, helping your account grow more quickly. Not participating in an employer retirement fund that offers a match is downright foolish since you are essentially passing up free money.

If money is tight, even small contributions will allow you to benefit from your employer's match. As you free up additional funds, simply increase your contribution.

As a side note, you should know that while you never lose the money you contribute to one of these employer-sponsored plans, some companies won't let you take their contributed funds unless you have been working with them for a set period of time. This period of time varies by employer.

But what about IRAs?
Traditional and Roth IRAs (Individual Retirement Accounts) can also be very significant tools for building a financial future. As I encouraged you to do on Day 36, start by investigating the retirement plan(s) your employer provides (if any). If your employer doesn't match your funds, an IRA may be a better option.

An IRA can be funded with just about any investment that you can think of (well, except maybe your collection of snow globes). That means that you can pick any stock, bond, mutual fund or CD in which to invest your money. (If you don't know what these are, don't worry, your financial advisor does and will lead you in the right direction.) IRAs differ from company-sponsored plans in that a company-sponsored plan may only offer you a few investment options. If you're interested in more information about IRAs, you should consult an investment advisor.

Sign up today.
Your task for today is simple: sign up. If your employer offers a structured plan such as a 401(k), start taking advantage of it as soon as possible. If your employer doesn't offer you a plan, consult with your financial advisor about starting either a Roth IRA or a Traditional IRA. I can't emphasize enough the importance of "early money." The very first dollars you put into a plan are the most powerful in that they are subject to whatever rate of return you earn for the longest amount of time. In other words, $1,000 put into your plan this year is much more powerful than $2,000 you put into the plan 20 years from now. Now, go after it and sign up. Today.

Day 38

Access More Income

Can you directly influence your compensation? Does your job allow you to translate harder work into higher pay? Do you have any idea how your employer makes decisions about the timing or value of your next raise? It may not seem important, but understanding *how* you get paid is an important step to solidifying your financial life.

Everyone should understand their compensation structure and the various ways they can increase their access to additional income at their current job. But there is another, less-discussed reason understanding your compensation structure is important. If you need more money for basic expenses and you can't directly affect your income at your current job, you may need to get a second job. This is a controversial but necessary solution in some cases. If you have made all of the behavioral adjustments outlined in this book including budgeting, controlling your spending and modifying your habits to optimize your cash flow, yet you still have a chronic shortage, it's safe to say that you simply need more money. More money is rarely the solution to chronic financial problems, but if you have exhausted all the other options—including taking drastic measures such as downsizing your house or car and selling material things that are outside of your means— perhaps it's time to get a second job or to find a way to increase your pay at your current job.

In order to increase your income, you will need to increase your focus, keeping your eye on the prize!

Making more money at your current job
Before you start looking for a second job, you should know that there may be ways for you to extract more pay from your current job. Since you are already attuned to the demands, policies and environment of your current workplace, you should look for the low-hanging fruit, i.e. new income streams from your current employer. An increase in income can come in many forms.

1. **A raise.** You would be hard pressed to find someone who doesn't think he or she deserves a raise. The real challenge is positioning yourself to get one. If you are undercompensated (compared to your industry peers and coworkers) or if you can document value, you have the justification to ask for a raise. Many people make the mistake of asking for a raise based on an arbitrary amount of time that has lapsed since their last raise—say, once every year. Sure, if you haven't had a raise since 1985, you can make a case for a raise based purely on the cost-of-living increases, but otherwise there's really no rule that says you deserve a raise every year. If you can't think of a reason you deserve a raise, your employer probably can't either.

2. **Special projects.** Are there special projects you could take on at your job to increase your compensation? Volunteer for them. If they don't exist, consider designing them. Not only will you potentially increase your pay, but you will also increase your exposure to new experiences and your stature and value within the company. Which might just put you in a place to ask for that raise...

3. **Goal-driven bonuses.** If you have the opportunity to earn bonuses based on achieving certain benchmarks—whether through meeting

sales goals or otherwise enhancing business for your company—make sure you understand the requirements. In my experience, many people fail to familiarize themselves with their companies' bonus programs and thus miss out on opportunities to contribute to their long-term financial goals. Some employers offer bonus opportunities on a monthly, quarterly or annual basis. I've seen many cases where almost 50% of a person's total compensation depends on hitting their bonus requirements, and other cases where it's possible for a person to more than double their annual income based on the same. Don't leave money on the table, especially if you are within striking distance of your bonus benchmarks.

4. **End-of-year bonuses.** Some employers offer holiday bonuses out of the kindness of their hearts, but usually there's a little bit of science behind this seeming benevolence. One reason for end-of-year bonuses is that employers need to get rid of some of their profit to avoid paying taxes on it. But the reason they offer bonuses is a lot less important than how they decide to divide the bounty among employees. Trust me, everyone at your company is not getting the same holiday bonus, meaning that these so-called "gifts" are ultimately based on *something*. If possible, find out what that something is and increase your some-thing-factor so that your boss increases your holiday bonus in return.

5. **Overtime.** If you get paid by the hour, it's very likely that you're eligible for overtime pay. Generally, if you work more than 40 hours per week, state laws mandate you get paid "time and a half." If you make $10/hour, you will begin making $15/hour once you hit 41 hours in a given week. Of course, allowing someone to work overtime isn't very economical to an employer, so there might be strict rules about this where you work. But if your employer is short on staff and needs you to fill in, consider volunteering to do exactly that.

On Day 39, we'll discuss overtime pay and bonuses in detail. In particular, we'll talk about why you should not depend on these things as part of your long-term financial strategy. Putting this money toward debt and other financial obligations to get yourself out of a hole, however, is a great way to put these opportunities to good use.

If you need more money for basic expenses and these options either aren't available to you at your current job or don't satisfy your monetary needs, your next step is to seriously consider getting a second job.

Getting a second job
A second job doesn't have to duplicate the nature or setting of your day job, nor is it likely to. Be creative: consider baby sitting, delivering pizzas, mowing lawns, shoveling sidewalks or doing anything else that brings in a few extra bucks. You aren't looking for a revenue stream that matches your day job (although that would be nice); you're simply looking for some extra funds to help you fill in the gaps. A second, part-time job should bring in couple of hundred dollars per week, which can go a long way towards getting you out of a tight spot or accomplishing your financial goals. No matter how nice that extra money is, however, you shouldn't make this a permanent part of your financial plan. A second job should only be viewed as a temporary solution. If you have to maintain a second job for more than two years, you are in need of a more permanent solution such as a career or drastic lifestyle change.

Today's task: If you feel certain you need additional incoming funds, figure out how much more money you need to get back on track.

(This activity isn't for everyone, but it is for anyone who has a constant budget shortage. If you still have a regularly-occurring shortage in your budget after Budget Week, you need to match up your shortage with a new potential source of income.)

If you have followed the tasks each day, and you are still short on money, you need to make more money without delay.

1. What is your typical monthly budget shortage? $ _____

2. You need to make sure your second source of income covers your budget shortage after taxes. In order to figure this out, multiply your answer by 1.25 to account for taxes. $ _____

3. How much more money do you need to make each month?
    $ _____

Whether you decide to focus on earning more money at your current job or getting a second job, additional income can go a long way in filling budgetary gaps. Because a second job can have all kinds of implications for your schedule and general well-being, make sure that you have truly exhausted all the other expense-cutting methods we've discussed before choosing this route.

Day 39

Manage Overtime and Bonuses

Overtime and bonuses can actually be burdens in tough financial times. If that sounds crazy to you, consider whether overtime and bonuses have made you more careless in your spending and less attentive to your budget than in the past. You must learn to view these rewards as additional and occasional in order to avoid financial failure. We touched briefly on overtime and bonuses on Day 38, looking at how they can be used to supplement your income in time of extreme shortage. Today, we're going to talk about how they can negatively affect you if you rely too heavily upon them.

We didn't always take overtime and bonuses for granted. It might surprise you, but the origins of the modern 40-hour work week can be found in a social campaign created by Welsh socialist Robert Owen in 1817. Owen's core belief was summed up by the slogan "Eight hours labour, eight hours recreation, eight hours rest," which was part of a larger social campaign for better working conditions. The battle over reasonable work hours continued to rage throughout the 19th and early 20th centuries in industrialized countries. By 1937, the 40-hour work week was so culturally established in the U.S. that the Fair Labor Standards Act mandated overtime compensation. Under the terms of this Act, a company is required to pay overtime on any time worked over 40 hours as long as an employee is not considered to have "exempt" status.

Three factors determine exemption: salary-based employment, specific types of duties (oddly enough, commercial fishing and newspaper delivery are exempt duties) and salary level. (A full list of exemptions can be found at www.WorkplaceFairness.org.) For the remainder of America's workforce, the moment an individual works more than 40 hours per week, he or she is compensated at 1.5 times the normal hourly pay rate for the excess hours. I've had clients who make up to $30,000 extra per year by working overtime. That's a lot of money, but here's the catch: it's not reliable. Unfortunately, it's all too easy for people to start to depend on this type of income, and that is what I want to address today.

You must learn to budget on your base salary (after taxes) alone. If this idea seems crazy to you, you may already be in trouble. Companies have granted overtime and bonuses so frequently over the last 20 years that many people have become accustomed to these additional sources of income. Yet many of these same people are now starting to panic. As companies tighten belts and look for ways to cut costs, Americans are seeing their opportunities for extra compensation evaporate. Suddenly, their expenses are outpacing their incomes.

The promise of additional pay can even be a problem for job-hunters. In some fields prospective employers tell prospective employees the base salary, but sell the job by revealing the average bonus or commission. This is exactly what happened to me when I was interviewing for my very first job. The company representative told me I would have a base salary of $30,000, but that my commission would likely catapult me into the $100,000 range within a year or so. That sounded great. Sadly, the reality was far different. The $100,000 range turned out to be the average of the entire sales department, which included many sales veterans. The newer salespeople pulled down the average, and my salary didn't end up being much higher than the base. Learn to be immune to this kind of recruitment technique to avoid negative consequences for your financial life.

Let's determine how susceptible you are to a dangerous bonus situation.

1. What is your projected total annual earned salary? $_____
2. How much of that is a base salary? $_____
3. What is the remaining amount? $_____
4. Divide #3 by #1: $_____

Your total	Your level of susceptibility
0.0-0.1	**Suitably stable.** You would still be financially stable if your hours, bonuses and commissions were cut.
0.1-0.25	**Slightly dependent.** You would need to make some adjustments to your spending if your pay were cut.
0.26-.50	**Dependent.** You either took a job that had a very low base salary, or you are dangerously overextended. Take a serious look at whether or not you are in danger of having your compensation reduced. Is your industry, company or department struggling? All the more reason to take immediate action and re-examine your spending.
0.51-higher	**Very dependent.** This is a serious problem, especially if your pay involves overtime. Many commissioned salespeople eventually end up with a skewed pay ratio like this, and despite the fact that it is the norm in their line of work, they are at risk as well. If more than 50% of your income is from bonuses and overtime, you need to keep your spending limitations constantly in mind.

Overtime and bonuses should not be used as a means of extending and expanding your existing budget; instead, treat them as investments in your financial future. Your extra compensation, no matter the magnitude, should be used for long-term financial priorities, not for day-to-day living expenses. Don't blow through your bonus frivolously, despite what others around you may do. Squandering a bonus or overtime pay on many little purchases is as bad as using it for everyday living expenses. Put your bonus in your emergency reserves or in long-term savings (for a down payment on a home, for example). Use your overtime money to pay off debt or to help fund college expenses. Do great things with this money. You won't regret it.

Day 40

Have a Career Backup Plan

Day 39 touched on how instabilities in your industry should force you to stop depending on your bonus and overtime pay. But do you have a plan for a worst-case scenario? What would you do if you were laid off? If you can't answer with specific details, you risk financial emergency. You shouldn't wait until you need a backup plan to develop one. Here are some simple questions that can help you anticipate and prepare for an involuntary career change.

- Are there better opportunities within your industry than those you have at your current job?
- Is your industry in decline?
- Is there another career you have always dreamed about, but have not pursued due to self-doubt or other reasons?
- Are you developing relationships with other potential employers?
- Does going back to further your education make sense for you as a long-term career step?

There aren't any right or wrong answers to these questions. But it is important that you answer them in order to give yourself a sense of where you stand. Your financial life needs stability, and you need honest perspective to make informed decisions about your present and future.

Regardless of your current situation, there are three key things you can do to prepare yourself for future instability.

1. **Update your résumé,** especially in a tumultuous employment climate. Keep it current and be sure to update your references. In addition, make sure your résumé is formatted according to current standards. Nothing hits a trash can faster than a résumé that looks like it came off your dot-matrix printer in 1986. Be sure that you are active (if it's important for your field) on LinkedIn and other professional sites.

2. **Join an industry association.** This is wise regardless of how you feel about your current job and even if you are looking for a new one. Staying up on your industry's latest trends is a must if you want to have a career backup plan, and you'll be forming a network of contacts who can help you land on your feet in times of crisis.

3. **Stay abreast of job postings in your industry.** I'm not suggesting that you constantly jump to the next "best" job, but I am suggesting that you take stock of your industry. This can add valuable job security, and it could increase your current income. (See Day 38: If you're underpaid by industry standards, you might just have a case for a raise.)

The hope is that you'll never need to put your backup plan into action. But the possibility of the unknown makes this exercise worth the time. As part of this process, you should not hesitate to evaluate yourself relative to peers in your field. This will give you a good basis from which to measure your marketability and a better understanding of how best to sell yourself.

Most importantly, developing a career backup plan gives you another opportunity to be proactive with your financial life and to maintain more control of your financial destiny. Individuals who simply react are more likely to be knocked down when life throws them for a loop. Don't be left behind: Planning and foresight are key to maintaining stability and to staying one step ahead of uncertainty.

Day 41

What to Do if You Are Laid Off

Layoffs happen for a number of different reasons, including poor company performance, poor employee performance or cost-cutting. If you are currently suffering the effects of a layoff and are prepared to think through your situation rationally, then you can mitigate these effects. Whether you think you may be subject to a layoff or not, Day 41 offers specific steps for making the best of a worst-case scenario.

If you're laid off as a result of your company's poor performance or because your company simply needs to cut costs, you may have more options than you think. You might even be able to save your job and help the company back to profitability. Always take active steps to control your destiny. Though you may not be successful, you should not accept a layoff as a foregone conclusion. If, despite your best efforts, you are unable to keep your job, you need to avoid some of the common mistakes people make when they face career uncertainty. I've seen people cash out retirement plans, ignore transferable benefits and leave unemployment compensation on the table. I'm sure the list of mistakes goes on, but I'm going to focus on the most essential lesson: how to come out ahead after a layoff.

After completing this day, you will be able to meet unexpected detours on your career path with a toolkit of strategies and a process for applying the tools in it. Day 41 is your guide to career triage.

1. **Don't panic.** People tend to freak out—and rightfully so—when their income is eliminated in an instant, but freaking out is a waste of energy. If you panic, it will only make it harder for you to formulate your contingency plan. In some instances, you may be able to salvage your job, but you will need to approach the conversation with composure. Additionally, you don't want to overreact and burn any bridges with your employer. There's always a chance you will get called back if the layoff is only temporary. Finally, panic can be interpreted as desperation, and we all know how attractive that quality is to potential suitors across the board: *not very*.

2. **Negotiate.** Were you in the middle of a massive project when you were laid off? Offer to finish the project on a freelance basis. Are you the only person who knows how to carry out a certain task for the company? Offer to write the operations manual. Make your employer an offer, and try to negotiate a role for yourself in the company. The more unique value you brought to your company, the higher your chances of success in negotiating with them. You may even be able to negotiate staying on at a reduced salary. Of course, before taking this step, you should consult your budget to see if that scenario would make sense for you.

3. **Immediately determine the implications of your job loss on your benefits.** We discussed your employee benefits in great detail on Day 36, but it is crucial to review them again after a job change. Your two main concerns should be your health insurance and your life insurance. You will most likely be offered the opportunity to continue your health insurance coverage temporarily under COBRA (Consolidated Omnibus Budget Reconciliation Act). COBRA makes it possible for you to extend coverage for 18 months, albeit at a higher premium cost. More details are available at the U.S. Department of Labor website (www.dol.gov).

As we discussed on Day 33, the problem with having all of your life-insurance coverage through work becomes evident once you lose your job. At this point, the term life insurance provided to you by your employer usually terminates because it is not considered "portable." You should contact a trusted insurance advisor immediately and secure term life insurance if you do not already have it. Many insurance companies will temporarily bind coverage—or make it available immediately–during the underwriting process if you make one month's payment at the time of application (pending health requirements).

4. **Do not cash out your retirement fund.** As the *Austin-American Statesman* reported in fall 2009, a Hewitt Associates study found that over half of 20-29 year olds cashed out their 401(k)s when they left their jobs. That's horrendous. When you cash out your 401(k) early, you have to pay taxes on it—plus a 10% penalty. Your 401(k) should not be part of your emergency plan. Do not touch it. Not convinced? Let's assume that your 401(k) balance is $10,000 at the time you are laid off. But due to your poor planning, you decide to cash it out. You would owe about $2,000 (20%) in taxes, plus an additional $1,000 (10%) penalty. In other words, you are paying $3,000 for a $7,000 loan. Cashing out really doesn't make any sense.

5. **Figure out for how long you can survive without income.** The answer is important because it gives you a delineated time frame for finding a new job. Ideally, you can make it for at least 30 to 60 days (although your emergency fund should cover you for up to three months without income). Cut out non-essential spending, recalculate your budget and apply the lessons that you have learned in this book. In particular, refer back to Week One, paying special attention to Day 2 ("Count Your Purchases").

6. **If eligible, apply for unemployment benefits.** You may qualify for unemployment benefits from your state. Every state has different qualifications for eligibility. Many states offer unemployment compensation for up to 26 weeks. This means that you can receive weekly compensation of up to a few hundred dollars while unemployed. You must adjust your budget to this new level of income. As we'll discuss in Day 42, try to supplement it with part-time income rather than becoming dependent on unemployment. Consult your state Department of Workforce Development for more details.

Getting back on the horse

So you lost your job. It's a stressful and scary situation, but I can assure you you're not the first person to go through it, and you won't be the last. So pick yourself up and don't for a second be tempted to feel sorry for yourself.

Amy Kopelan—creator of The Guru Nation (www.thegurunation.com), a career-advancement and networking website—agrees that finding a job in tough economic times requires exhausting a number of resources. Here are some of her strategies for an effective job search:

1. **Sign up to attend industry events.** As we discussed in Day 40, this is a great way to get noticed by and network with people who can influence your career options. Even better, volunteer to work or manage these events. You probably won't get paid, but consider it an investment in your future.

2. **Consider employment in fields that don't represent your dream job, but do keep you connected to the industry that you want to work in.**

3. **Attend free seminars with industry leaders.** Collect business cards and note the websites, Twitter handles and LinkedIn profiles of people with whom you can build a relationship and continue to network. If you don't know about LinkedIn and Twitter, it's time to learn. Social media tools are a great way to develop your career network.

4. **Entertain job offers for a lower salary than you normally would.** If you're frustrated by the thought of having to take a pay cut to stay employed, set a goal to steadily move toward a new position. If you've taken a job as a stopgap measure in a field you don't necessarily love, establish a date for yourself (maybe one to two years) by which you will find something else in the field of your choice. As with many situations, regaining control of your career path depends on your ability to set and meet specific goals.

Regardless of what happens, know that you have the financial skills to handle this challenge. You *will* get back on your feet, and you *will* meet your financial goals. It may take longer than you expected, but you have mastered the fundamentals and now know what's important.

Day 42

The Glory of a Part-Time Job

Stay employed. Stay *very* employed. As we discussed on Day 38, a part-time job is a great way to get a leg up on your financial goals—whether you have just been laid off, or if you simply need additional income.

A part-time job can significantly change your financial life:

1. As a primary source of income after a job loss.
2. As a mercenary mission to fund a financial goal.

1. **A part-time job as a primary source of income after a job loss:**
   If you were to lose your job, your employer might give you a severance package. This package can be a flat amount of money or it might even offer supplemental income for a set period of time. While both options can be helpful, I've seen these benefits in practice several times and rarely do people use them correctly. Allow me to paint a picture.

   I had a client who had worked for a pharmaceutical company for 12 years when he received notice that he was to be laid off. His company offered him severance income for the next six months, which was great, but the job market was soft and the prospect of finding a similar job was slim. My client looked at his severance package as a means of taking his time to find the perfect replacement job. He continued living his normal lifestyle as the six months quickly passed by. Not surprisingly, his severance income ran out and he was stuck without a new job. He began accumulating debt at the alarming rate of $1,500 per month. What, exactly, was his mistake?

He should have secured a part-time job during his job search. He could have saved all of this new income and bought himself more time. Instead, he wasted a great opportunity to secure his financial life in an already difficult time.

Don't kid yourself, looking for a job is NOT a full-time job. Never sit on severance income. Always add to it immediately. This may go against your pride, but it simply makes sense.

2. **A part-time job as a mercenary mission to fund a financial goal:** Do you have an attainable financial goal that you're not making much progress on? It could be your lack of focus, or it could be that you don't have enough dedicated income flowing into the project. Getting a part-time gig can solve both of these problems.

Take this example. You need $2,000 for your 10th wedding-anniversary trip to London, but you can't seem to fit it into your current budget. If you refuse to alter your plans or are unable to stretch your budget to come up with that $2,000, a part-time job can be a good solution. Think of it as "homemade overtime." Following are some part-time jobs that will help your bottom line. But don't be fooled, just because these jobs are attainable on a part-time basis doesn't mean they don't require skills. If you can't rely on your current skill set to find a part-time job, make an effort to learn some new skills.

- Bartender
- Waiter
- Banquet server
- Coffee-shop barista
- Lawn care
- Snowplow driver (seasonal)
- Food delivery
- Floral delivery
- Data entry
- Tutor
- Baby-sitter

Have you crunched your budget six ways until Sunday but still can't find room for everything? Are you running in place on your journey towards your financial goals, despite living lean? Are you wasting severance pay? If you said yes to any of these scenarios, it's time to consider whether a second job could help you move beyond your current circumstances.

Week Seven

Develop Savings Habits

You do realize there's a very important reason you're doing all of this hard work, right? That reason is cash flow. Yes, all of the cash you've saved will ultimately go toward your financial future. This might not sound as fun as buying a new sports car, but this really is great news! There's nothing more luxurious than not living paycheck to paycheck and being able to fund life's pleasures without relying on other people's money (debt). Can you imagine pre-funding your vacation? Your next car? Or your retirement? All of these things can be achieved through the combination of hard work and discipline with the proper savings habits.

In Week Seven, we're going to develop a savings plan and hash through the many, many reasons why your savings is an important part of the overall financial mix. You'll learn how to save money in the short-term, mid-term and long-term. You'll get the lowdown on the dos and don'ts of picking a trusted advisor who will help guide you through this process. Finally, we're going to have a serious sit-down chat about your investment patience. Take a deep breath and say your *Om*s, ladies and gentlemen; this is going to be an exciting week. Enjoy it. You've earned it.

Day 43

The Importance of Savings

Defining financial success is challenging. Does *having* a great deal of money make you a financial success? Not exactly. You could have obtained the money without actually earning it. Does *making* a lot of money make you a financial success? Not in and of itself. If you spent every dime you made, you would actually be considered a financial failure. Does having the appropriate amount of savings for any situation that may arise make you a financial success? Now we're talking. The fact of the matter is that financial success has very little to do with how much money you have or earn. But it can be measured by your financial efficiency with the assets or income you have. In other words, it's not what you earn, but what you keep. It's all about savings.

People who regularly save money tend to be better problem solvers. They realize that you can address problems before they occur simply by having extra financial resources available as a result of careful saving. If you haven't figured it out already, your financial life is all about problem solving. Everyone faces financial puzzles and challenges, but robust savings will allow you to solve them on your own terms.

How big a role do savings play in your life?

Yes No

1. ☐ ☐   Do you have enough saved for your next vacation?

2. ☐ ☐   Do you have enough money saved to buy gifts for the next holiday?

3. ☐ ☐   Do you have savings in place to fund your next major purchase?

4. ☐ ☐   Do you have savings for your next housing purchase?

5. ☐ ☐   Do you have enough money saved for routine maintenance on your car?

6. ☐ ☐   Do you have enough money to survive unemployment for at least a month?

7. ☐ ☐   Do you have enough money to pay your insurance deductibles?

8. ☐ ☐   If you own your home outright, do you have enough saved for your property taxes?

9. ☐ ☐   Do you have enough money saved to cover your next income tax payment?

10. ☐ ☐   If you received an invitation, would you have enough money to participate in your friends' weddings or other important celebrations?

Maybe you haven't thought about situations like these but you should. People sometimes struggle when they try to save money because they don't have specific goals. Saving is much easier when you are doing so for a specific goal or purpose.

Today's task could possibly change your life forever. Today, you will stop finding reasons you can't save and just start saving.

Here's how: log in to your online banking and set up an automatic transfer from your checking account to your savings account. Set up the automatic transfer to take place in the same amount each payday. If you aren't currently doing this, start by deciding how much you should transfer each payday. If you have no idea how much you can afford to save each month, first consider each of the following scenarios and determine with which one you most identify.

1. **You know that you waste money.** This means that you refuse to think about small adjustments in the present that will have a big impact in the future. If this is you, you need to take an aggressive stance. For example, if you think that you waste $300 per month, you need to automatically transfer at least $150 into savings over the course of the month.

2. **You don't think you can afford to save.** If you've made it this far in *60 Days to Change*, you are now likely in a position (or working toward being in a position) to put money toward your financial priorities. Now you need to get started, even if that means saving a nominal amount of money. Start by saving $20 per paycheck via an automatic transfer to your savings account, and then see if you can increase it over time.

Whether you think you can afford to save money or not doesn't matter. You can, and you can start now. Think of it this way: you can't afford *not* to save money. Committing to saving money each month is the most powerful exercise in this book. Savings are valuable for two separate reasons that are equally important: they prevent you from wasting money and they accumulate money for your future. Don't lose sight of that.

Day 44

Adjust Your Savings and Investment Risk

Planning for the future is the key to your continued financial success, but if you make the wrong investment you risk financial ruin. (Yes, I'm trying to scare you here. Is it working? Good. Financial ruin *should* be scary.) Different types of investments offer different degrees of risk. Generally speaking, and ranked from degree of least risk to greatest, common investments include:

- **Bonds**. You should think of this security-representing debt as a very official "I.O.U." If you hold a bond, a person or an organization is obliged to pay you money.
- **Mutual funds.** Professionally-managed pools of money that hold stocks, bonds and cash.
- **Stock.** Ownership interest in a company.

People make investment decisions based on past average investment returns, and the financial industry perpetuates the notion that past returns are good indicators of future performance—yet many investments are not repeat successes. How in the world does this make sense? It doesn't. Open any money magazine and you will see mutual-fund advertisements celebrating amazing rates of return. The devil is in the details, though; as the small print confesses, past performance is no indication of future performance. Moreover, the wrong people often take the wrong degree of investment risk. Pre-retirees are involved in investment portfolios with a high degree of risk, and people who are hardly out of their first job sink what should be long-term savings into unprofitable, get-rich-quick stock schemes. Those near retirement definitely shouldn't be playing fast and loose with their savings, and just because you're young enough to handle the ups and downs of a volatile market doesn't mean you should.

So, what type of risk should you take? Well, there are two main components to understanding risk. First, assess your personal risk tolerance. How much investment risk can you handle? Do you lose sleep at night thinking about how your money is being invested? If so, then you likely have a low level of risk tolerance. Generally speaking, you can afford to invest your money at a higher risk level when you are between 20 and 48 years old (so long as the risk involved is not due to the fact you're investing in a get-rich-quick scheme rather than a legitimate investment!). If you're older than that, then you probably need to reduce your risk tolerance.[*]

This brings us to the second component in understanding risk. Always keep your time horizon in mind. Know how long you have before you will need the money you're investing. The closer you are to needing it, the less risk you should take. For instance, if you know people near retirement who just lost a great deal of money in the stock market, they are now likely suffering the consequences of not keeping their time horizon in mind. The stock market is too risky a place to keep your money when you're so close to retirement. Likewise, parents of small children and pre-teens should be aware of their time horizons in deciding how aggressively to invest college funds. If parents lose money in the market while their children are teenagers, it can be financially devastating considering the limited time for financial recovery.

---

[*] This is not meant to be specific investment advice.

Investing your money doesn't have to be complicated. If you can remember and apply the following two rules of thumb, you should be fine:

1. Don't adopt a level of risk that causes you to lose sleep.

2. The closer you are to your target date, the more you need to lower the risk associated with the investment.

If you ignore these two simple rules, you could end up an example in my next book like poor Vince and Tessa, who were on the verge of retirement and financial disaster when I first met them. Vince had worked as an electrician for 41 years, and Tessa worked for the local Humane Society. Their retirement income was supposed to consist of Social Security income, a pension from the electrical workers union and the income that they could generate from their 401(k)s. Vince hadn't changed his investment options in his 401(k) in nearly eight years. While his investments weren't risky per se, they were risky given his time horizon. If his portfolio were to suffer any losses, he wouldn't have the proper amount of time to recover.

Fortunately, I was able to help Vince and Tessa before the market tanked in 2008. We reallocated his retirement savings into fixed-rate investments that prevented him from losing money. Since he already had enough money for retirement purposes, there was no need to put his money at unnecessary risk. All we had to do was lock in his portfolio so that he wouldn't lose any money as a result of shifts in the market.

Think of risk like baseball. If all you need to do is get to first base, then don't try to hit a home run. Swinging for the fences when all you need is a simple hit is too risky.

Let's examine how your investments relate to your time horizon. Below is a list of traditional financial goals. (If your goals aren't listed, please add them.) List how much time is left until you need each set of funds, and how much you have saved for each goal.

Goal	Amount saved	Length of time until you need it
College funds		
Down payment on a house		
Retirement		
Child's wedding		
Car		
Other		

The most important concept you should gather from this day and exercise? The closer you are to needing your money, the less you should put at risk. Leaving your money at risk for too long can have serious consequences.

Whether you're an adrenaline junkie or just feeling particularly "young and risky," if you are within two years of needing access to your money, you have no business putting your money at risk.

Day 45

The Three Tiers of Savings

As you conserve for the future, you need to create three categories of savings: short-term, mid-term and long-term. We have already discussed the importance of short-term savings—the category also known as an emergency fund—but we've yet to fully explore the other two tiers of savings.

Mid-term savings generally fund large purchases like cars, houses and education. It can take years to build up mid-term savings, but the wait is well worth it. For example, instead of taking out a car loan, a good mid-term savings will allow you to pay cash for your car. The same idea goes for most other large purchases.

Long-term savings are even more critical because they continue to work for you when you stop working. Yes, we are talking about retirement savings.

"These days, retirement can last 30 years or longer, so you need to accumulate enough savings to last you for decades."

Did you know that you would need nearly $1 million saved to provide you an income stream of $50,000 per year in retirement (based on a 5% rate of return from a diversified portfolio)? Therefore, you must start saving for the long-term immediately, if you're not already. The best place to start is your employer-sponsored plan, as we discussed on Day 37.

As we discussed on Day 43, your savings plan must include automatic transfers from your checking account directly into the appropriate savings account(s). (You can set up multiple automatic transfers to cater to savings accounts representing each savings tier.) Always contribute first to your short-term savings account. That way you will be able to deal with the small financial emergencies that life might deal you. If you start saving long-term money first, you risk going into debt when an emergency hits. Oddly enough, the next account you should focus on is the long-term savings account, which is typically where you are saving for retirement. As I've mentioned before, the longer your money sits in your retirement account, the longer it will eventually work for you.

This doesn't mean you should ignore your mid-term savings. Quite the contrary, your mid-term savings is the most accessible of all three accounts and is most relevant to your daily life. If your emergency fund is full and you're regularly putting away money for the long term, your mid-term savings represent discretionary funds that you can use more freely to support your lifestyle. I would, of course, suggest you be prudent with this money, spending it with the same level of caution that allowed you to save it in the first place.

Remember that you need to drop coins into three separate buckets, short-term, mid-term and long-term. Start with the short-term bucket until it's filled (with three months' worth of expenses). Then begin contributing at least 10% of your net monthly income to long-term savings. Once you've established a regular schedule of deposits into long-term savings, you can begin filling the mid-term bucket. As you learn to work within your budget, you should increase your contributions to both your mid-term and long-term accounts. The goal is to increase your long-term savings investments to 15% of your monthly net income and to put all surplus cash flow into mid-term savings.

At a bare minimum, you should be saving at least 10% of your monthly income on a regular basis, and this money should be accounted for in your budget. As you may recall from Week Four (Budget Week), you should do this regardless of your debt level. If you don't, you risk going deeper into debt if a financial emergency strikes. Based on how much you have accumulated, then decide what percentage of savings to put toward each of the three tiers. If you've filled up your short-term savings, you can divert your money to mid-term and long-term savings.

Saving for an emergency, a major new purchase or for retirement is critical to financial well-being.

How much have you saved so far?

Day 46

Choose a Bank

Do you view your bank as a commodity? Do you assume that all banks are created equal? Do you have any idea what services your bank offers that other banks don't, and vice versa?

The purpose of these questions is not to stump you or even to quiz you. It's a means of getting you to begin thinking about the different roles banks can play and what types of things you should be aware of when selecting yours.

Let's start off by examining what you consider to be a bank's role.

True	False	Item
☐	☐	My bank should hold my money and then give it to me when I need it.
☐	☐	My bank should help me buy my house.
☐	☐	My bank should help me start a business.
☐	☐	My bank is a lifelong financial partner that should help me every step of the way.
☐	☐	My bank should provide me with a credit card.
☐	☐	My bank should be able to help me with my business's payroll and taxes.

Your answers to these questions will help us determine where you should bank.

These days, very few large banks offer only the "traditional" banking that consists solely of deposits, loans and withdrawals. Large banks have become a type of "financial flea market," in that they have everything and want to sell all of it to you. This isn't necessarily a negative thing (unless you have a thing against flea markets), but it may not make sense to those who aren't looking for a bank to handle much more than daily transactions. The main takeaway here is that big banks want to participate in every aspect of your financial life. If this interests you, you should be with a big bank.

Small or regional banks tend to be in the traditional banking business, meaning they cater primarily to customers who believe a bank should hold their money and give it to them when they need it. In my experience, smaller banks tend to offer better customer service than big banks (more my observation than a fact). That said, "better" or "more personalized" service is what people have come to expect from smaller banks. At least that's what I've gathered from my work in the financial planning trenches. Small banks also tend to do a better job underwriting risk, meaning that they don't grant as many loans. Because they are smaller, they have to stick to a very strict lending model. They can't afford loan defaults, and therefore they aren't as generous with their money.

Do you want your banker to know your name? Or do you want your banker to be able to handle any financial task no matter what it is? I'm sure there are some banks that *can* do both, but I haven't seen a bank that can *consistently* do both.

Take a look at the following table and rank, 1 to 10 (1 is most important and 10 is least), the order of importance of each of these banking services to you.

Rank (1-10)	Bank Services
	Personal relationship with a banker
	Large number of bank branches
	Easy-to-use online banking
	Ability to have your mortgage, investments and bank accounts in one place
	Low fees
	Low-cost or reimbursable ATM fees
	Excellent telephone customer support
	Online bill pay
	Online budgeting software
	Access to commercial lending (for your business)

Banking is many different things to many different people. Your sense of the value of these different characteristics will help you prioritize your banking needs. Take this list to your bank (or a different bank) and see if they offer what you're looking for. You will be surprised how inept some banks are at satisfying some of these basic needs. But knowing this will no doubt help you eliminate a few from consideration. You pay for your banking one way or another, and you should make sure that you are leveraging those fees against services that are important to you.

Day 47

What to Look for in a Financial Advisor

Financial advisors come in many shapes and sizes, but it's hard to find one who has everything you need: knowledge, the power to motivate and an honest desire to help. The good news is that they are out there. You just need to know what to look for to find them.

First, at what point should you be looking for a financial advisor?
It's simple. If you're currently running in place financially, you need a financial advisor. If you have money in the stock market, you need a financial advisor. If you're saving diligently for retirement, you need a financial advisor. If you have a pulse, you need a financial advisor. My point? Everybody needs a financial advisor. If you're broke, a financial advisor can help you become *un*-broke. If you're wealthy, a financial advisor can keep you that way. You just need the right kind of advisor with the right characteristics.

What is the role of a financial advisor?
The role of financial advisors has changed drastically over the last several years. Whereas the financial advisor pool was once primarily comprised of stockbrokers and insurance professionals, it has evolved to include a sea of financial planners and money coaches. Because there are so many options out there, there is a lot of room for error for consumers who are trying to choose an appropriate advisor. And beyond having too many options,

consumers often don't fully understand their own needs. Many times this combination leads them to choose the wrong type for their situation.

A good way to simplify is to base your decision on your primary concern. If your primary concern is investments, you should choose a money manager. If your primary concern is putting together a financial plan, you should work with a financial planner. But no matter what type of advisor you choose, you need to make sure that that person has the qualities that give you the best chance for financial success.

What should you look for when choosing a financial advisor?

Knowledge. Your advisor should have a good understanding not only of the financial markets but also of personal finance. This tends to disqualify many financial advisors, as most either know something about investments, insurance or personal finance but rarely know enough about all three to be of value in each aspect of your fiscal life.

The ability to motivate you. A good advisor has the ability to work with you to produce the results you desire and to help you perform better than you may think possible. You need to seek out someone who is willing to ask you the questions he or she needs to fully understand your goals. Someone who believes in these goals should work with you to increase your motivation to achieve them. Finding someone who can achieve the latter is especially important—the ability to inspire motivation is a unique talent that separates the good advisors from the majority. Think of your relationship with your doctor. If your doctor tells you to stop smoking, but then leaves it at that, he/she isn't really offering you much in the way of inspiration. But if your doctor were to tell you why you should quit smoking, offer you a plan to do so and then check in on you regularly to gauge your progress, he or she is not only demonstrating belief in your goals but also offering you additional inspiration to achieve them.

A true willingness to help. Some financial advisors possess tremendous knowledge and motivational powers but just won't help you because you don't fall into their "ideal client" demographic. Very few financial advisors are compensated in a way that encourages them to help everybody, not just people with lots of money. Many big brokerage firms won't even help you unless you have a certain (large) amount of money to invest. Your goal is to find someone who is willing to help you regardless of the amount of money you have to invest. This is challenging but definitely possible. Interview candidates from several firms, and make sure that when you do, you pay more attention to the advisor you meet than the overall philosophy of the firm. Needless to say, there are good and bad eggs at every financial institution.

How are financial advisors compensated?
Advisors are usually compensated via commission or fees, and there is a debate in the financial services industry as to which pay structure results in more objectivity. Many feel that fee-based planners will give you the most unbiased advice because they aren't trying to sell you anything. They are paid a flat fee to consult with you about your finances. I disagree with the assertion that a fee-based compensation structure always results in objectivity. On the flip side, just because someone is selling you something doesn't mean they are being less than honest or disregarding your best interest. I've seen terrible fee-based planners and terrible commission-based advisors. Ultimately, I wouldn't focus too much on their compensation structure; I would focus more on the three crucial characteristics I outlined above.

How should you go about finding the best financial advisor?
As I said before, it's difficult to find an advisor who possesses each of these traits. Not only are they a rare breed, but the compensation structure of the financial industry just doesn't support it. The financial industry's inability to truly help the people it serves is a harsh reality.

Just as you would do before hiring any other service professional, you need to do your research and ask around. Ask your coworkers if they are happy with their advisors. Search online to find advisors or go to small business networking events.

Three pointed questions to ask a potential advisor
Lists of questions to ask financial advisors have been around for years, but I find that most of the questions on these lists are lame. And by "lame," I mean that they don't get to the core of the matter or help you gather the information you really need to make an educated decision. Based on my experience and assessment of what one needs in an advisor, here are the questions you can and should ask:

1. *Tell me a situation in which you have taken a client like me and helped him or her increase financial net worth.* Don't let advisors off the hook here. They need to illustrate how they plan to take someone with your available cash flow into the promised land.

2. *How will you help hold me accountable to my financial goals?*

3. *Who is your ideal client? How much money does an ideal client make and have? Do you have many of these clients?* Based on this answer, you may find that you are nowhere close to being a match for this advisor. Then again, you could be perfect. If their ideal client is not you, you'll know it.

Finally, don't begrudge your financial advisor's right to make a living, but keep in mind that his or her ability to earn commission should not come at the cost of your financial success. If your financial life has not been enhanced by your relationship with your current advisor, you need a new one.

If you're able to find an advisor who meets the criteria I've outlined today, snatch him or her up! If you can't find a good fit right away, know that you can also start to build your financial future on your own. You will need a working knowledge of the financial industry and a desire to change, but you can get to work now.

Day 48

Pre-Fund Financial Goals

There is no better feeling than completely pre-funding a financial goal. This way, the purchase date comes and goes without incident. You avoid incurring debt or affecting your credit score, and you can move on with your life. So, can you pre-fund all of your financial goals? It's doable, as long as you understand the following rules.

1. **First things first: Be flexible.** You must be willing to delay the time of purchase if you haven't properly funded the goal. Even if you have done everything else correctly, a lack of flexibility will hinder your efforts to pre-fund your goals. (And if you can't be flexible, you should skip straight to #5.)

2. **Start saving early.** The earlier you set the goal, the sooner you will be able to start saving for it. Did you know that the most important money you save is the first money you save? It's not a riddle; it's the truth. Let's say you invest $100 every month for five years at 5%. The most valuable portion of this investment is the $100 you invested the first month. Since that $100 was subject to the 5% compounding interest (meaning that you earn interest on interest) for the longest amount of time, it will naturally grow the most. This should encourage you to focus on investing early, rather than investing as much as possible. Early money produces better results.

3. **Be realistic.** Your income must be able to support your goals. It would be unrealistic for someone who makes $50,000 per year to save $30,000 in one year. But in some cases, it's possible to save one entire household income while living solely on the income of your spouse or partner. I've seen this work numerous times and in many different income situations. I had a client who made $75,000 per year while his wife made $115,000 per year. Instead of increasing their lifestyle, they saved her *entire* income. Make sure that your income and time frame support your dream.

4. **Don't get aggressive with your savings.** When you're trying to pre-fund a goal, make sure you're using only a savings account or a money market account (a type of high-interest savings account) as the vehicle. Pre-funding your goals becomes difficult when you're constantly (or even just sometimes) losing money due to aggressive investing. You can open a money market account at almost any bank or financial company. Just make sure to look for one that doesn't issue fees or penalties for withdrawals.

5. **Be a financial mercenary.** On Days 38 and 42, you considered the possibilities that a second job could offer. Doing freelance work, selling the products of a hobby like woodworking or jewelry-making or having a garage sale are all ways of finding and creating opportunities that will allow you to reach your financial goal more quickly. This isn't necessarily about finding a second job; it's about streamlining your life and finding the proverbial change in the sofa cushions. Even simple projects like digging through your garage for things to sell on Craigslist or eBay can result in more than you might imagine. (I made $400 in one weekend this way and cleaned out my garage in the process.) You are selling yourself short if you are looking at your primary income as your sole source of revenue. If the goal is important to you, you can find ways to make additional money (legally, obviously).

The bottom line is this: pre-funding a financial goal is not always the easiest solution, but it is certainly one of the best. Make a chart (on your computer or simply on a piece of paper) that can help you track the progress toward your goal. This will motivate you and allow you to monitor your progress.

Day 49

Develop Investment Patience and a "Percentage Perspective"

My father was (and still is) one of the most influential figures in my life. One of the most important things he ever taught me was that "patience is a virtue." According to my father, it's simple: chill out. The same can be said of how you approach your investments: learn to be patient.

Pop quiz.

What is 50% of $1,000?

$500.

Correct.

What is 5% of $10,000?

Also $500.

The fact that the answer to both of these questions is $500 is the very reason that impatience often accompanies investing. In my experience, many beginning investors have unrealistic expectations about investment returns. When they find out the truth—that returns are more likely to be around 5% than 50%—they can become discouraged. This has a lot to do with the fact that people view money in terms of immediate dollars instead of long-term percentages—a perspective that can cloud their ability to evaluate the effectiveness of an investment. On Day 49, I'm going to help you reset your perspective on investments.

Let's say for a moment that you give me $1,000 (your life savings) to invest. Most beginning investors get anxious about locking up (or making illiquid) their long-term savings. I don't blame them. I was anxious, too, the first time I invested. But here's the problem: 5% (which is an arbitrary, but not entirely unrealistic, amount that I've chosen for the purposes of this example) of $1,000 is only 50 bucks. For some, giving up access to $1,000 for an entire year only to earn $50 stinks. Many expect something better, like $500. But think about it: that's 50%, which is a very unrealistic (maybe even delusional) return. And that, my friend, is why investing requires patience *and* the right perspective.

Your patience is a critical component of your financial success. Of course, success is relative, as is $500. Growing wealth takes...*time*. But as Americans who are accustomed to a 24-hour news cycle and to having access to *everything* on demand, patience is a rare commodity. One way to manufacture it, however, is by employing the 40-30 rule.

What's the 40-30 rule? It's the concept that it takes 40 years of work to fund 30 years of retirement. That's patience. As someone who is decades away from retirement, I find the prospect of waiting 40 years to retire daunting. But it is reality for most. And I don't mean reality-show reality. I mean *real* reality. It will take the average 22 year old 40 years to build up enough money, retirement benefits and Social Security benefits (assuming they have access to these) to retire. I don't know about you, but that scares the hell out of me. Forty years to provide you with 30 years of relaxation. But it makes sense.

And during those 40 years of saving and investing, you have to continue to fund your life, which saps your economic resources, and that is one area where your patience can tangibly pay off.

Your patience reality check
Your realistic expectations about investment returns can help you develop investment patience.

1. How much money do you have to your name, right now?
   $_____
   (This number will be your baseline for rest of the exercise.)

2. If you were to double this amount of money over the next 10 years, it would equal a 7.2% average rate of return. If you doubled $1,000 over 10 years, you probably wouldn't be especially impressed. But if you doubled $100,000 over 10 years, you most certainly would. The reality is that in both cases you have experienced an annual rate of return of 7.2%.

3. If you were to get a 5% rate of return over 10 years on the amount of money that you listed for Question #1, how much money would you have? $_____

4. Would the dollar amount gained impress or affect you?

Your ability to keep things in perspective is paramount to your success. Start looking at your investment returns in terms of percentages instead of dollars, especially in the first few years of investing. Investment patience allows you to truly appreciate the fruits of your labor. Maybe my kids will write a book one day and say that their dad used to have a saying, "Look for the percent sign, not the dollar sign." I can see it now.

Week Eight

Major Purchases

An important part of making significant financial change revolves around your preparation for future big-ticket purchases. *60 Days to Change* has spent the last seven weeks teaching you how to deal with daily financial decisions. But this week we are going to focus on the importance of planning major future purchases. You don't just wake up in the morning and decide to buy a house (at least, I hope you don't). Deciding to buy a house is a long process, and this week you will learn how best to think through the process of making this kind of major financial decision.

Major purchases should never be spontaneous. I'm not trying to take the fun out of consumerism; this is simply a mantra you should adopt in order to consistently do the prudent financial thing. Planning major purchases doesn't necessarily mean that you have to cut back on the purchases themselves, but that you should take the time to consider the ramifications of committing major dollars to major buying events. This week, we will walk through this process.

Day 50

Plan Your Next Purchase

There are two types of mistakes that can ruin you financially: big ones and little ones. Little mistakes, such as overspending on dining out and constantly incurring overdraft fees, seem insignificant because they involve a relatively small amount of money. But consistent little mistakes have the ability to make a big impact over time in that they chip away at your financial progress.

Little mistakes can be signs of bad habits, and these habits can be quite challenging to fix. Believe it or not, big mistakes are easier to fix than the small ones. It all starts with understanding how to make a big purchase. This week is all about how to avoid making the wrong decisions about the major purchases in your life.

So what type of purchases am I talking about? To start, your home and car purchases (which I will discuss in detail throughout the week). We'll also consider a major purchase anything that costs more than 20% of your net monthly household income. For example, if your net monthly household income is $4,900, I consider anything that costs more than $980 to be a major purchase for you. Eye-opening, isn't it? Depending on your situation, major purchases could be televisions, kitchen appliances, computers, mountain bikes and lots of other fun things.

Let's take a look at a very common scenario: the purchase of a flat-screen TV. The process of buying a high-end TV is the perfect example of a major purchase that could potentially go wrong. Doing it right requires research, budgeting and patience. Doing it wrong results in an impatient impulse buy. If you want to buy a TV in late fall, wait until the best deals appear—on Black Friday (the day after Thanksgiving) or the day after Christmas. Impatience could cost you a few hundred dollars. A flat-screen TV purchase isn't necessarily a bad idea, but you must take the proper steps to ensure you can afford it. (And remember, not being able to afford something isn't a bad thing.)

"Being able to say "I can't afford it" is a positive thing."

How can you identify past big purchase mistakes so you can avoid them in the future? Here are the top three things to think back on when evaluating the prudence of a particular purchase.

1. **Did you open a store credit card?** Yes, I know that you may have saved 10% on your purchase by applying for the store credit card at the time, but at what cost? Did you carry a balance on that card for any length of time? The new credit card certainly affected your credit report. If you had to take out a credit card in order to make the purchase, you shouldn't have made the purchase in the first place.

2. **Did your purchase cause an argument?** If your purchase caused financial stress for someone else in your household, this may be a sign that you made a mistake. Over the years I have seen this happen many times. One person makes a major purchase decision without consulting (or in spite of) their partner. Have you ever been the victim or the instigator of this situation? It's not fun.

3. **Did you find yourself over-justifying your purchase?** Are you still making a case for a past purchase, yet no one is listening? Then you are likely over-justifying something that you shouldn't have bought in the first place. Evaluating your past purchases takes a great deal of self-awareness and honesty. We have all made purchasing mistakes, and if you are still trying to rationalize a past purchase, it may be a sign that the purchase was a mistake.

Identify past major-purchase mistakes

So what is it? The car you bought? The motorcycle you never ride? Don't be ashamed. Just be honest. We have all made mistakes, including me. When I think about the purchase of my first home, I know that I made a mistake. I should have rented. I broke even on the sale of the home, but I would have been better off renting and investing the difference. Knowing and admitting this has helped me improve my financial habits. Now it's your turn.

What are some of your past major-purchase mistakes? List three examples below, and look for patterns in your purchasing logic (or lack thereof).

1. _____

2. _____

3. _____

Was it the magnitude, or timing—or something else entirely—that turned these purchases into mistakes? Did you create urgency where there wasn't really any? As you look at any patterns that emerge, try to pinpoint why and where you went wrong. How would you approach each purchase differently, equipped with the strategies from the last seven weeks?

To make sure you don't repeat your past ills, be sure to employ these three strategies the next time you consider making a big purchase.

1. **Research.** With the advent of the Internet (thanks, Al Gore), research has become quite easy, as has price shopping. As you research, identify and rate how important these three factors are for you: price, quality and service. With a decreased price usually comes a compromise of quality and service. How much are you willing to compromise? Researching a buying decision helps you evaluate your preferences.

2. **Save.** Want to know one of the best ways to determine whether you can afford a major purchase? Already having the money to make the purchase. This doesn't give you carte blanche, but it does eliminate the possibility of paying interest on a potentially poor decision. And if you have saved for a major item over a period of time, you have had plenty of time to consider the prudence of the decision to buy it.

3. **Be patient.** Walk away and think about it. Pressure can often drive you to make a poor buying decision. Being patient can prevent you from making impulsive purchases that could damage your financial situation.

Regardless of what you intend to purchase, these three tips can help make any buying experience more fruitful for you in the end. Don't give into impulse; be strategic. It's simple: by researching, saving and being patient, you will never go wrong.

Day 51

Your Home: Buy or Rent?

If you are like the majority of Americans, your primary expense is housing. The cost of housing in the U.S. is often between 20% and 50% of net monthly income. The optimal figure is 25%. I say "optimal" because 25% isn't always realistic based on your income or location. If you have rented for a long time, you may be itching to buy a home. But take the long view first, and evaluate the affordability of buying versus continuing to rent.

According to a 2009 Realtor.com study, the average 2008 home value in the U.S. was $196,600.[1] This particular number shouldn't necessarily play too large a role in your decision to rent or buy; it's just a point of reference. The real determinant of your home's affordability is that home's location. For example, the same study revealed the median price for an existing home in Chicago in 2008 to be $245,600, whereas the median price for an existing home just a few hours away in Lansing, Michigan was $97,700. These staggering figures help illustrate the classic real estate adage, "location, location, location." But your ability to pick a "location, location, location" really depends on affordability, affordability, affordability. As you know by now, this concept plays a fundamental role not just on this day but throughout *60 Days to Change*.

---

[1] For more information, go to www.realtor.com.

These housing statistics should help you understand above all that buying a home isn't for everyone. It might have made sense in the 1950s, when the variation of housing prices based on locale wasn't as significant as it is today. But housing booms in some parts of the country can now make owning a home virtually impossible for the average Joe. Do you live in San Francisco and make $100,000 per year? Good luck trying to buy a house: the median home price in San Francisco in 2008 was $622,000. In that case, renting is not only your only option, but it is the smartest option, too.

Some terms to know

Down payment: the amount of money you provide to your mortgage holder during the initial purchase of a home. This money is your initial equity. We will discuss down payments in more detail on Day 52.

Equity: the amount of your home that you actually own. For instance, if you live in a home for which you owe $80,000, and the home is worth $100,000, you have $20,000 worth of equity. You own $20,000 worth of your home. Equity can increase as you pay down a mortgage or as the value of your home increases relative to the amount you owe on the mortgage. Increases in equity can also result from home improvements, additions or an increase in the real estate market.

Mortgage: the contract between you and a lender for the purpose of purchasing a home. In other words, a home loan. A typical mortgage contract lasts 15 to 30 years.

Interest rate: for the purposes of Day 51, this refers to the rate of interest that you pay on your mortgage. Most mortgages are amortized over 15 or 30 years, though you pay the majority of the interest to your lender early on. In fact, approximately 25% of the total interest paid over a 30-year loan is paid in the first five years of a mortgage.

Factors to consider when making a housing decision

1. **Can you afford to buy a home?** This question is the best place to start. There are many other factors in evaluating your ability to buy a home, all of which we will cover in great detail on Day 52, but this is the most important one.

2. **Can you afford to own a home?** Owning a home is more work than making the decision to buy a home. You might qualify for a home loan to purchase a 150-year-old home, but you might not be able to afford the upkeep and maintenance costs involved in owning a house this old. In addition, utility costs and regular maintenance concerns make owning a home quite expensive, compared to renting a home. A good rule of thumb is to budget 1% of your home's value for annual upkeep. If your home is worth $300,000, for example, you should budget $3,000 per year ($250 per month) for maintenance.

3. **How long are you going to stay in one location?** Most Americans move every five to seven years, so buying a home is generally inefficient. The problem is magnified if you are in a stagnant real estate market. You can gain equity in your home in two ways: by paying down the principal on your mortgage (not including interest payments) or by increasing your home's resale value. If resale prices aren't increasing and you aren't paying down the principal, you aren't increasing your equity. At a 7% mortgage rate, 85.29% of your total house payment for the first five years will go to pay interest. In other words, less than 15% of those mortgage payments will go to increasing your equity. You are, essentially, renting your home.

4. **What are the pricing trends in your area?** Like many assets, home prices tend to rise in value over time. This varies by location, however. Familiarize yourself with the pricing trends in the area

you're interested in. It doesn't make sense to buy a home in a market with falling home prices, whereas it certainly makes sense to buy a home (all things considered) in a rising real estate market.

Are you in a position to buy a home or are you currently in a home that you can afford? To find out, let's evaluate whether you are better off buying or renting your principal residence.

Down Payment
Can you make at least a 10% down payment on the home?
Yes_____   No_____

Or, if you currently live in a home, do you have at least 10% equity?
Yes_____   No_____

Income
What is 25% of your net monthly household income?_____

30-Year Fixed Rate Mortgage Affordability Table

Mortgage rate	$100,000	$200,000	$300,000	$400,000
7.5%	$699.21	$1,398.43	$2,097.64	$2,796.86
7%	$665.30	$1,330.60	$1,995.91	$2,661.21
6.5%	$632.07	$1,264.14	$1,896.20	$2,528.27
6%	$599.55	$1,199.10	$1,798.65	$2,398.20

Mortgage value

Looking at this table and considering the price of homes in your price range, can you realistically say that 25% of your monthly household income will go toward paying your mortgage, based on a 30-year fixed-rate payment at 6.5% (or slightly more)? [2]

Yes_____   No_____

Don't let this table get you too excited, though. We will be discussing mortgage affordability in great detail on Day 52. There are *many* other factors to consider besides the affordability of a 30-year fixed-rate payment. This particular exercise is simply meant to help you decide whether to even enter into the mortgage discussion.

Job Stability

Has your industry been relatively immune to layoffs historically?

Yes_____   No_____

Are you in good standing at your company?

Yes_____   No_____

Utilities and Maintenance

Utilities and maintenance typically cost an amount equal to 30% of your mortgage payment. Can you afford this additional cost?

Yes_____   No_____

Property Taxes and Insurance

Property taxes and insurance costs can turn an otherwise good housing decision into a bad one. These costs vary greatly based on location. Have you researched what they would be for your prospective new home? Can you afford these additional costs?

Yes_____   No_____

---

[2] You can check current mortgage rates with your mortgage broker or bank. I am only using 6.5% as an example.

Don't guess the answers. You owe it to yourself to determine to what extent each of these factors (monthly payment affordability, down payment, income, job stability, utilities, maintenance and property taxes and insurance) influences your housing decision. If you answered no to any of these questions, you need to rethink home ownership at the current moment.

How does renting compare to buying?

According to a 2006 report from the Harvard University Joint Center for Housing Studies, over 80% of all people 25 years old and younger rent, and over 66% of people ages 25 to 29 rent.[3] For an entire generation renting seems like the smartest option. Why? Renting is almost always cheaper due to the additional costs of owning a home. If you can't afford to be saddled with either monthly or long-term mortgage costs for at least another 5 to 10 years, renting is your best option.

By now, it should be quite obvious to you whether to buy or rent. Just because you're qualified to buy the home, doesn't mean that you can actually afford it. As I've mentioned several times, past lending standards have caused many people to take out mortgages on homes that they couldn't afford. You may need to talk to a real estate or mortgage expert to determine if you have any better options. But if you *are* in the position to buy a home today, what next questions do you need to consider?

---

[3] Source: "Fact Sheet: America's Rental Housing—Homes for a Diverse Nation", Harvard University's Joint Center for Housing Studies, March 08, 2006.

Day 52

How Much Home Can You Afford?

If you have concluded that buying a home is the best thing for you, the next thing you need to evaluate is how much home you can afford. If you already own a home, this is a prime opportunity to evaluate the money that you have allocated towards living there. Is your current home costing you too much?

Deciding to buy a house, townhouse or condo should be a long-term goal. Give yourself plenty of time to prepare for the mortgage application process. In the year prior to applying for a mortgage, you need to pay off as much debt as possible, save for a down payment on the home and research the ancillary costs of living in the area where you have chosen to buy your home.

There are a number of different types of mortgages and home loans, but if you want to be completely sure that you can afford one, look into a 30-year fixed-rate mortgage. There are a number of different mortgage types such as adjustable-rate and interest-only mortgages that require lower payments than a 30-year fixed-rate mortgage, but if you *have* to rely on these types of loans, it could be because you truly aren't able to afford home ownership. Don't get me wrong—you can use these different types of loans, but make sure that you can afford the 30-year-fixed mortgage.

When you obtain a mortgage, your lending institution will typically require you to make a 20% down payment, which protects the institution in case you default. If you are unable to pay your mortgage, the bank will keep your down payment because they are stuck with your house. If you are unable to put 20% down, you will be required to pay Private Mortgage Insurance (PMI), which insures your bank against your default. PMI is a waste of money. I would rather see you take out two separate mortgages than agree to a PMI plan. A more acceptable situation would be a 10% down payment, a loan for 10% of the purchase price and a loan for 80% of the purchase price. A single mortgage company will not want to loan you more than 80% of the purchase price without PMI protection. But by breaking your loan into two separate loans, you eliminate the need for PMI, and the interest deductions from the second mortgage reduce your tax burden. Better still, you can deduct the mortgage interest of your primary residence on your taxes. (Consult with your tax advisor to see how this affects you personally.)

You will be tempted to find ways to afford the home of your dreams. But you should set a firm cap on what you can spend, and then work backwards. Don't depend on a future increase in your income to help make your house more affordable. Sometimes those increases just don't come, and even if they do, they don't always make their way to your mortgage payment.

On Day 51, I mentioned that ideally your monthly housing costs will not exceed 25% of your net monthly household income. If you follow this rule of thumb, it is unlikely that you will ever risk owning "too much home." But the secondary and tertiary costs of owning a home often get people in trouble. These additional costs are what truly affect how much your home will cost you. When making a housing decision, you need to take into account a variety of factors that will eat into your short-term and long-term housing budget, including property taxes, home insurance, maintenance costs, homeowners association dues and utilities.

Housing costs breakdown

1. What is the amount of your current or proposed mortgage payment (principal, interest, taxes and homeowners insurance)? $ _____

2. Annual maintenance for your home will typically cost you about 1% of the total value of your home. What is 1% of the value of your home? $_____

3. What is the monthly cost? (Divide the previous number by 12) $_____

4. Do you (or will you) have homeowners association dues? Yes_____ No_____

    If so, how much are they/will they be per month? $_____

5. You should typically budget an additional 30% of your mortgage payment for utilities. For instance, if your monthly mortgage payment is $1,000, then you would budget an additional $300 for utilities (including phone, gas, electricity, water, waste, TV and internet). What is 30% of your mortgage payment? $_____

    Add all of these numbers up. What is the real monthly cost of your housing choice? $_____

The final figure above should not exceed 35% of your net monthly income. If you can fit all of your housing expenses into your budget for less than 35% of your net monthly income, you can afford your housing decision. A variety of factors can make the decision more or less affordable, but if you are right at 35%, you have greatly reduced the risk of experiencing housing-related financial difficulties.

One last point: most mortgage lenders will let your mortgage payment be 28% of your gross monthly income. Don't do it. Lenders are in the business of selling you a home loan, and some will try anything possible to give you a loan. This includes loaning you more money than you should borrow.

Stick to the *60 Days to Change* numbers: a maximum of 25% of net monthly household income for your housing payment and 35% of net monthly household income for total housing expenses.

Day 53

Your Car: Buy or Lease?

Buying anything new is exciting, but you would be hard pressed to find many things more exciting than buying a new car. Ahh...that new car smell, that sparkling finish, that crafty finance manager... Huh? You didn't know that the finance director of a car dealership is all part of the experience? Well, then, we have a lot to cover.

Buying a car is not like buying a sandwich (this observation alone is worth the price of this book). If you happen to be walking by a deli and you get a certain hunger tinge, you'll likely saunter into said shop and buy a sandwich. Your limitations are quite simple: You either have the money to buy the sandwich or you don't. There's no built-in system that helps your sandwich dreams come true. And if there happened to be a guy who sat in a dark office with the sole purpose of making you a sandwich-owner today with a smile and a handshake, you would probably run. (And, yes, I realize you technically *could* put the sandwich on your credit card, but just pretend that's not the case, so I can keep this example here. I happen to love the image of a weird sandwich finance guy sitting in a dark room.) Ahem, back to the car...

So what's different about buying a car? Typically, the missing factor in buying a car is your own affordability awareness. When you buy a sandwich, you know whether or not you can afford it. When buying a car, many people genuinely have no clue. And that is only the first mistake. You need to make many decisions before you ever set foot on the lot. These decisions include how much car you can afford (how much the monthly payment will be), how much your down payment will be and, finally, whether you should buy or lease. This last decision will certainly affect your entire budget. But we'll get to all the details of buying a car on Day 54.

The option to lease a car has met some bad publicity in the financial world: many experts feel that leasing is inefficient. Generally speaking, I tend to agree. But leasing a car can be a brilliant way to avoid endless payments for a car you don't want to keep for the long-term. *Consumer Reports* reported that 27% of all new vehicle acquisitions in 2007 were leases.[1] That's because leasing simply makes sense for some people. Let's figure out if you're one of them.

The first decision you need to make is whether to buy or lease. Look at the following descriptions of a typical car lessee and a typical car buyer and decide which one best describes you.

Typical car lessee
- Drives relatively few miles per year (fewer than 15,000 per year)
- Consistently wants a new and/or different type of car every few years (Is this your vice?)
- Needs an affordable short-term solution
- Insists on always having the car covered under warranty
- Takes very good care of the vehicle

---

[1] Source: "Comparing auto-financing options: How to decide whether a loan or a lease is more economical for you," www.ConsumerReports.org, April 2008.

Typical car buyer
- Drives an average to high amount (15,000 miles or more)
- Wants to have no car payment eventually
- Has a greater level of patience with an older car
- Doesn't feel the need to always drive a new car
- Prefers to customize the car

Which category best describes you?

An oversimplified way to approach this is to decide if you are someone who insists on always driving a new car. If so, you should consider leasing. Frankly, I don't think that anyone *needs* to always drive a new car, but I'm not going to waste my time trying to convince you that driving a new car doesn't make sense. This would go against my advice from Day 19 ("What's My Vice?"). If your car is your vice, that's your decision.

Leasing is definitely a worthwhile option for some—but before you commit to it, you should ask yourself the kinds of tough questions you now know to ask before making financial decisions. Do you really need to lease? Could the funds be better spent, or saved? Is there room in your budget for a lease? If the answer to many of those is no and if you are the average person who just needs a reliable set of wheels to go to and fro, you should be buying, not leasing, a car.

Day 54

Your Next Car Purchase

Even if you have determined that your car is your vice and that you want to buy rather than lease, this doesn't mean you should go wild; you will still need to make an intelligent decision. Whether you decide to buy with a loan or take a lease-to-buy option, the goal should be to pay for the car as quickly as possible. Stretching out a car loan or committing to a longer lease is a bad idea. Longer contracts mean less flexibility, and less flexibility means that other financial goals don't get the attention they deserve. You might be tempted to spread out your financing in order to lower your monthly payment, but the real solution is to buy a less expensive car.

The ideal situation is to bypass a car payment altogether by pre-funding the purchase. This might mean buying a used car or a less expensive one, both of which are far better options than the alternatives: getting locked into high monthly payments or buying a car you can't afford. But I do realize that pre-funding isn't always possible. Here's how to make a car-buying decision that won't destroy your entire budget.

To start, don't finance a car for longer than five years (three is ideal). It would be nice to buy a brand new car, but when you try to fit your transportation costs into your budget, you will probably have to make cuts somewhere. So, consider buying a certified pre-owned car, a relatively new car that is still under warranty from the manufacturer. Buying a certified pre-owned car strikes the right balance of frugality and practicality. Don't focus solely on the affordability of your car payment. (This holds true whether you buy or lease.) Consider *all* of the costs involved in transportation (gas, maintenance and insurance).

You should keep your total transportation costs between 10% and 15% of your net household income, regardless of whether your household needs one or two cars. If your take-home pay is $35,000, your maximum payment should be approximately $3,500 ($291 per month), and your total transportation costs should be 15% of your net monthly household income, around $5,250 per year.

These may seem like severe restrictions, but if you want to spend more on transportation than prescribed, you will need to make the proper changes to your budget. In other words, feel free to spend more, but know you will need to make significant cutbacks in your budget to allow for this.

Let's see how transportation costs affect your current or future driving situation.

What is your net monthly household income? $_____

What is 10% of your net monthly household income? $_____

What is 15% of your net monthly household income? $_____

How do your current transportation costs compare to this number? Let's take a look, starting with monthly costs.

Current car payment: $_____

Current monthly fuel cost: $_____

Current monthly insurance cost: $_____

Total monthly costs: $_____

Now, your current annual costs.

Maintenance: $_____

Oil-change costs: $_____

Tires: $_____

Car washes: $_____

Repairs: $_____

Total maintenance: $_____

Monthly maintenance (the total above, divided by 12): $_____

Do you have to keep your transportation costs below 15% to be a financial success? No. But you must be willing to adjust your spending in other areas. On Day 43, I recommended that you save 10% of your income (a line item that should not be sacrificed). On Day 52, I told you that you shouldn't spend more than 35% of your income on total housing costs. With your savings, house and car, you potentially commit 60% of your income to only three areas of your life. And if you don't make tough choices, that 60% of your income can easily creep toward 80%. When that happens, you have lost control, as the savings component is nowhere in sight. The more you spend on big purchases, the less you will be able to save for financial priorities.

Day 55

Avoid Buyer's Remorse

Have you ever been really excited about a purchase but at the same time felt guilty about it? If so, you've experienced buyer's remorse, which is cased by a cognitive dissonance (the feeling that results from two simultaneous but conflicting ideas). When it comes to your purchases, this cognitive dissonance can be described in two sentences: "I'm glad I bought that," and "I can't believe I just bought that." Buyer's remorse can result from purchases large or small, but usually the larger the purchase, the greater the remorse.

We've all been there. I know I have, and I learned that it's easy (and sometimes convenient) to confuse buyer's remorse with dissatisfaction. For example, let's say that I buy a new watch. Once I get the watch home, I realize that it isn't the high-quality watch that I thought I was buying. That's dissatisfaction. On the other hand, if I bought the watch and, once home, begin doubting the prudence of the purchase, that's buyer's remorse. The dissatisfaction in the first example could have been prevented had I done better research ahead of time, but basic critical thinking could have prevented the buyer's remorse in the second example.

Buyer's remorse is, quite simply, a product of asking the right questions at the wrong time. Critical analysis of major purchases should be made prior to purchase, not after when the euphoria of acquisition has worn off.

Most people think that buyer's remorse is a bad thing, but buyer's remorse is one of the best things that can happen to you. It means that you have common sense. We have all bought something that we shouldn't have: a dinner out, a TV, a car or even a house. The cognitive dissonance that takes place when you regret how much you spent means that your brain has a pulse. And that's a good thing since it means you can avoid this feeling in the future. You simply need to ask the right questions at the right time. Here's what you should be asking *before* a purchase:

1. Have I thoroughly researched my potential purchase?

2. What is the alternative to not making the purchase?

3. Am I creating an artificial deadline? (Could I live without this item for another month, two months or six months?)

Think back over the last 12 months, and identify five purchases that brought on a case of buyer's remorse. Analyze what the underlying financial issues were, and what would have been a reasonable alternative to making the purchase.

Purchase	Why did it bring on buyer's remorse? (What financial cues was your conscience trying to give you?)	What would have been a reasonable alternative to making the purchase?
1.		
2.		
3.		
4.		
5.		

60 Days to Change will force (and ideally already has forced) you to look back on some of your past spending transgressions and identify alternate solutions. Buyer's remorse usually results from buying what you want instead of buying what you need. There is nothing wrong with buying things you want. You just need to be strategic about how you plan for and afford these purchases.

Day 56

The Finances of Furthering Your Education

Few things are more important than education. Education allows us to learn about the world, ourselves and others. Most importantly, it teaches us to think critically, which allows us to make better decisions. What better way to test our decision-making skills beforehand than to make a decision about how to fund an education?

Based on the Digest of Education Statistics for 2008 (produced by the Center of Education Statistics), over three million Americans received post-graduate degrees in 2008.[1] This means that approximately 1% of Americans received a post-graduate degree in 2008. That is quite impressive.

I am a proponent of continuing your education throughout your life, and there are various ways to do this. Some of the challenges of funding your education, however, can result in financial advantages and disadvantages. Today, we will explore both to help you make...you guessed it...an educated decision.

Is it possible to be over-educated? Absolutely not, but it *is* possible to allocate too many of your financial resources to education, thereby over-paying for it. The ultimate question is really how much to invest in lifelong education (as a means of increasing your general awareness and knowledge of the world) and continuing education (as a means of career advancement and increased salary potential).

---

[1] Source: nces.ed.gov/programs/digest/d08/

How do you measure how much you should spend on education? It really depends on why you're furthering your education.

Education can be a means to an end, as is the case when one goes to school to train for an opportunity to make more money. Or it can simply be a way of gaining more knowledge for the sake of learning.

Although this is a book about money, you shouldn't assume that I am a proponent of education solely for future financial gain. In fact, I am all for allowing your passions to guide your career and educational decisions. As this book stresses, however, you must consider the financial ramifications of any major decision, and that includes education.

In challenging economic times, many Americans turn to education as either a time filler while they remain unemployed or as means of learning new skills to position themselves ahead of the competition. But education costs a great deal of money. According to Finaid.org, graduate students typically borrow between $30,000 and $120,000.[1]

That's a lot of money. And if you are going to spend or borrow money like that, you need to have a plan. Remember that furthering your education is not always a sure indicator of future financial gain, so proceed with caution and thought. Take the time to understand all of the financial implications of a decision to further your education.

Debt, in its absolute essence, is all about leverage. A mortgage allows you to leverage your income for the benefit of a principal residence. But what are you leveraging the debt from education against?

Your ability to earn money. At some point in time, as a working adult, you must leverage your education against something.

---

[1] Source: http://www.finaid.org/loans/

I had a client who sold his insurance business and decided to go to nursing school. Although he accumulated $20,000 in student loans, he was able to leverage this debt to make more money as an emergency-room nurse. More importantly, he was doing something he loved. He specifically chose a field of study that had a high demand for highly-skilled workers. If you too can leverage your debt to advance your income and career, education will prove to be a wise investment. But as I said before, future financial gain is not the only reason to go to school.

So what are the questions to ask yourself about the economics of furthering your education? Here are some good ones:

1. If you are going back to school to improve your income or job prospects, how high is the demand for jobs in the field of study you are entering?

2. Can you work and go to school at the same time?

3. Can you pay for your education as you go? This would eliminate the need for student loans.

4. Can you afford to pay back your student loans within 10 years of graduating? For instance, $50,000 in student loan debt (without interest, for the purposes of our discussion), paid over ten years, would cost you $416.67 per month.

5. If you are not furthering your education for the purpose of creating a better financial situation, do you have a plan to pay back the cost of your education?

So this is what I ask of you: do not consider a post-graduate education a compulsory event on the road to further employment or re-employment.

A $75,000 graduate education matched up with a $30,000 salary makes for tough financial times. I am not asking you to give up your dreams, but I am asking you to weigh value. Do you know how long it would take you to pay off a $75,000 education loan on a $30,000 salary? This is a trick question. Most student loans are for 10 years. That means you would have to pay at least $625 per month (not including interest). But on a $30,000 salary, that is over 33% of your net income. It might be time to reconsider your plans or look for more affordable options (can you take night classes while you work?).

Education is important, but at what cost? Enlightenment may be priceless but an education has a price tag. You should seriously consider this cost. Your financial future is much more fragile than you think, and you need to take an objective view. It can be the difference between a good 10 years of financial progress, or a difficult 10 years of sacrifice and challenging cost-cutting measures.

Week Nine

Devise a Permanent Plan for Success

This is it. Week Nine ties together the final pieces of *60 Days to Change*. But this isn't a throwaway week. Far from it. These last few days are like the final hours of a home renovation, when you're running around to tighten bolts and screws, touch up trim paint, make sure everything is functioning and do final inspections. If you made it this far, you've done more than clean your financial house. You've rebuilt it.

As with any renovation, you'll stand in the new space and marvel at what it used to look like. Think back over the last eight weeks. The way you think about money has changed drastically. You can probably name ten ways in which you approach spending, savings and financial goals differently. But don't stop there: Week Nine challenges you to kick any remaining bad habits and adopt new, good ones.

Week Nine gives you a bird's-eye view of the changes you've made—and gives you strategies for keeping them firmly in place for a long time to come.

Day 57

Get Rid of Bad Habits for Good

You're in the home stretch. In the last few days of *60 Days to Change*, it is vital that you give up any remaining bad habits. You have learned a tremendous amount about your financial life, but lingering bad habits can undo all of your great progress.

Maybe you have heard of the "21-day myth," the myth that it takes 21 days to develop a habit. With a little research, I learned that it takes much longer than 21 days to form or break a habit. According to a paper published in July 2009 in the *European Journal of Social Psychology*, it takes much, much longer to form a new habit: 66 days, on average, though the actual length of time depends on how intense the habit is.[1] Whereas it may only take 21 days to get into the habit of brushing your teeth twice per day, it may take an entire year for you to get into the habit of running two miles every day. With almost 60 days of personal-finance work under your belt, you're now perfectly positioned to make lifelong habits of the strategies we've discussed.

---

[1] Source: "How are habits formed: Modelling habit formation in the real world." *European Journal of Social Psychology*. 16 July 2009.

The main habit that I want you to take away from *60 Days to Change* is financial awareness. But there are numerous opportunities in this book for you to form new habits, and I hope you paid special attention to these days and weeks in particular:

☐ **Day 2:** Count Your Purchases

☐ **Day 9:** Repair and Build Credit

☐ **All of Week Three:** Control Monthly Spending

☐ **Day 22:** The Mechanics of a Budget Meeting

☐ **Day 43:** The Importance of Savings

If you ever get off track, going back to these days should give you specific ways to refocus since they emphasize the fundamentals of basic financial savvy. But the habit-forming shouldn't stop with those particular days. While each day gives examples of healthy financial habits to master, they are just the beginning. By all means, form new financial habits, but more importantly make sure you take the time to eliminate bad habits. Here are some things to consider as you do:

1. Let buyer's remorse clue you in to a bad habit. Although it doesn't feel good when it happens, it is a good thing and can tip you off to your bad habits.

2. Are you able to identify bad habits but don't have the self-discipline to change? Face your bad habits head on. Don't ignore them. Write down your bad financial habits, and hang this piece of paper on your mirror or refrigerator. Your bad habits shouldn't be a secret. Get them out there and start attacking them.

3. Adopt good habits. Put your loose change in a jar every day when you get home. (You can even mark the jar for a specific purpose such as a vacation or your anniversary dinner.) Use online banking to check your accounts on a regular basis. Hold a monthly budget meeting. New good habits will help shine a light on bad habits.

Nothing can keep you as accountable as a partner (or spouse, or friend), who can help you develop new (and good) habits. Clearly express your intent to change for the better and then focus on building together.

Day 58

Charity on a Budget

Now that you are well versed in how to budget and save wisely, you have probably found that you have a surplus at the end of the month. One of the best ways to show appreciation for this abundance is to give to others. And that is why thinking of and providing for others is part of *60 Days to Change*. You have learned inexpensive yet powerful ways to enhance your life: now pass it on to others.

When it comes to charitable giving, it's important to get into the habit as early as possible. But "giving" doesn't have to solely involve money. Plenty of people and organizations need time and resources too. Donating goods and volunteering are all ways of giving back, and nearly every organization is happy to have the help.

Chances are you're probably already active in many of the ways below, but if not here are a few charitable habits that have far greater value than the few dollars it takes to invest in them.

1. **Clothes in, clothes out.** Every time you buy new clothes, donate older clothes that you no longer wear. I haven't looked through your drawers or closets, but I'm pretty sure you have clothes that are just gathering dust. Moreover, if you have a basement or attic full of unused but serviceable

items, you have an opportunity to help your local Goodwill or Salvation Army. Your old clothes, home furnishings or appliances (all in good condition) could be real finds for someone else.

2. **Volunteer.** There is no more economical charitable activity than volunteering. And it doesn't require your money, just your talents and time. Do you love playing the guitar, but have nowhere to play? Check out local music therapy programs. Do you love kids? Consider being a mentor. Channel your passions and talents in helping others.

3. **Participate in a local school's Career Day.** High schools need people from all walks of life to describe their careers to the students. Students need exposure to different professions, and any input you can give them is great. I used to love Career Day. Without a doubt, the most interesting speakers were the firemen and truck drivers (in case you were wondering).

4. **Be a canned-food-drive superstar.** Shop from your own pantry, or make a visit to your grocery and buy from the list of needed items. Giving food is so much better than giving money, in my opinion. That's because it requires you to actually, physically do something rather than just write a check, which can feel like a chore. Next time you go to the grocery store, buy five to 10 cans of food. It will cost you about $5, which is not a large expense when it comes to keeping others in mind.

None of these suggestions involves lots of money, but they do require a fair degree of selflessness and awareness of other people's needs. Helping others is not a costly enterprise, and with relatively simple acts you can make big differences in your community.

Day 59

Know When and How to Act

A side effect of learning to manage your money is developing the confidence you need to make smart decisions in the face of temptation. And whether you know it or not, over the last 58 days you have established a tremendous amount of financial confidence.

You've learned some invaluable skills that put you at a distinct economic advantage over your peers, and you are now better prepared than most for the financial speed bumps—and even road blocks—that life can present. With this newfound preparation comes the end of ignorance. You will no longer be able to use the excuse, "I didn't know that." Nor will you feel comfortable asking the question, "How was I supposed to know that?" You now know *exactly what to do*. And now that you know *what* to do, you must learn when and how to act.

As you have learned, good things happen when you make better choices, like choosing to forego a few days' worth of lunches and coffee in order to afford one memorable dinner out, to assert control over your budget on a weekly basis and to examine (and then make the most of) your employee benefits. These are all examples of having the confidence to make a wise choice about what used to seem like a mundane decision.

Although you may now know what to do, you may also find that the best response has not yet become instinctive. If your instincts aren't working when you're faced with a tough money decision, there are key questions you can ask yourself to help you make a wise decision:

1. **How much will this really cost me?** Financial commitments and decisions usually don't end the moment after they occur. Each financial decision is either a stick or a tree. A stick has no roots—just a beginning and an end. A tree has roots that you can't see—tangled, complicated and numerous. Some financial decisions are self-contained (sticks), but other decisions have long-lasting ramifications and secondary commitments (trees).

2. **Where's the fire?** Why are you in such a hurry to make your decision? People tend to put deadlines on financial decisions: "I have to have this new mountain bike right now, or [fill in the blank]." The alternative to buying something is simple: it's *not* buying something. Don't make it bigger than that. If you have to justify your purchase, ask yourself if you really need it. Is your purchase really that urgent or are you manufacturing urgency? Don't create pressure situations that simply don't exist.

3. **Can I get a second opinion?** I'm not suggesting that you ask permission to make a financial decision, but feel free to solicit the opinion of someone whose judgment you trust. You need people who will give you objective, honest feedback. Go to this source when you temporarily lack the confidence to make a financial decision on your own.

Rest assured, you now know what you are doing, you have the confidence to do it and you can act accordingly. Don't be afraid to make financial decisions. Think back over *60 Days to Change*, and make sure that the decisions you are trying to make are in keeping with the principles and strategies. Making financial decisions can be difficult, but trust in your new skills and know that you can do it.

Day 60

You Made It!

Congratulations! You're just one step away from completing *60 Days to Change*!

Each person who has completed the *60 Days to Change* program has gotten something different out of it. The program began as a TV series on a variety of news stations across the country. I worked with families and individuals who knew that something had to give in their financial lives, but they needed that extra ounce of encouragement to make it happen. Viewers who watched along at home and visited the show's website came forward in droves to admit to facing the same ongoing battles with their finances. I received daily emails and letters from people across the country who had had significant financial breakthroughs and credited some, if not all of them, to the lessons you've learned these past two months. No matter how many notes I received, I was always amazed at how different each person's breakthrough was from the next. Now it's time to figure out what *you* got out of it.

To do that, we're going to complete one final exercise. (Hold your applause!) This chart is a way for you to critique your progress—to fully grasp the extent of your growth, to embrace your shortcomings and to celebrate just how far you've really come. Maybe these questions will even help you plan your *next* 60 days. What's in store? Financial expertise? Financial mastery?

Financial perfection? Let's find out, shall we? Take some time to reflect on each question. You may even want to thumb back through the text as you think about your answers.

1. What are you most proud of having accomplished during *60 Days to Change*?

2. On which day (or during which week) did you feel changes begin to take place in your spending, budget and/or financial outlook?

3. Was there one lesson that stood out as particularly illuminating?

4. What was the easiest part of *60 Days to Change* for you?

5. What part was the most difficult?

6. Did your communication about money matters with your significant other improve over the course of this program?

7. Has your financial acumen increased?

8. Has your financial confidence increased?

9. Do you feel more financially aware and adequately equipped to make more informed and discerning spending decisions?

10. Are you better able to handle financial emergencies?

11. In which areas do you know you still need help?

12. What is your next financial goal and how do you plan to go about meeting it?

So how did it go?

This time around, I'm not going to tell you what your answers mean. You have all the tools you need to assess your own financial situation. I pass to you the financial torch. This doesn't mean you won't continue to face financial challenges. Rather, when you do, you will know how to address them. Applying the lessons you have learned will allow these 60 days to jump-start your financial future. Keep this book handy so that you can refer back to it when you need additional inspiration or even more information to make the best decision possible.

What is *your* success story?
I haven't met one person who hasn't gained at least *something* from this curriculum, whether that something led to a huge financial breakthrough or whether it was a small tip that had the power to make a big impact over time. I mentioned earlier that I've been lucky enough to receive notes about different people's success stories. And every story I hear reinforces the fact that each person gets something different out of the program. How do your successes compare to these?

One woman, Natalie T., was able to formulate a plan to pay for two years of college for her son. Within the first three weeks of *60 Days to Change*, she found that she could save $500 per month; with that, she began building her son's college fund. At $500 a month for 15 years, she will be able to save $90,000—and that doesn't even account for the interest she'll earn along the way.

Jim K. lost his job during his *60 Days to Change*, but the skills he learned in Week Six allowed him to get back on his feet quickly. He approached his old employer and offered to head a project as an independent contractor. The project went so well that they rehired him as a full-time employee.

Annie and her husband Brett were able to work on the quality of their money communication, which helped them formulate a budget together and plan for the future. Instead of her being forced to handle the monthly budget duties all by herself, they began to have regular budget meetings during which they both took responsibility for their budget. They were able to discover an important financial empathy for each other that ultimately allowed them to understand each other's point of view on several non-finance subjects. Annie told me it was the best thing that ever happened to their marriage.

Kyle P. developed the strength and strategies to face his debt head on, and he no longer ignores situations that pose financial risk. He had fallen victim to his bad habits, and as a result, he had become complacent about the small things, like the fact that his poor credit limited him from even being able to open a checking account. Instead, he had been cashing his paycheck and living on cash. He was financially stagnant prior to his *60 Days to Change*, but he has grown steadily ever since.

There are many more stories like these, and I want to hear yours as well. Email me any time at pete@60DaysToChange.com.

I've had faith in you every step of the way, and I can't thank you enough for having faith in me over the previous 60 days. I hope that by giving me 60 days of your life, you have gained strategies and tools for a lifetime of good financial fortune. You can always visit my website, www.PeteThePlanner.com, to learn about additional ways to take control of your financial life.

Until next time we meet, remember: money rarely has anything to do with money. It's all about your habits.

Acknowledgements

Before *60 Days to Change* was a book, it was a television news program, website, financial-industry curriculum and radio program. When WISH-TV (CBS) in Indianapolis profiled families who were taking control of their finances with the help of my "*60 Days to Change*" program, thousands of people were inspired to sign up online for the free curriculum. They and their success stories were what prompted me to write this book.

WISH-TV (CBS), the station that originally produced "*60 Days to Change*," the genesis of this book, is a first-class organization, and everyone there was a pleasure to work with. I especially want to thank Stacy Thorne, the assistant news director; reporter David Barras; and photojournalist Joe Starlin. Thanks also to Jeff White, Kevin Finch, Joy Dumandon, Scott Sander, Eric Halvorson, Jason Crundwell, Deanna Dewberry, Dawn Clapperton, Janine Garner, Marissa Cotten, Scott Hainey, Tara Burmis and everyone at the station who helped get this giant project off the ground.

This project was originally the brainchild of Raquel Richardson and me. Raquel is a fantastic business partner with a brilliant marketing and design sense. Thanks to her and her team: Clay Mabbitt and Angela James.

I also owe a special thanks to my right-hand woman, Beth Weingart, my office manager and client coordinator extraordinaire. Beth helped keep my financial-planning business running during this project, and I don't know what I would do without her.

I would also like to thank my beautiful wife, Sarah, for her support and understanding. This entire project was taking shape at the same time that we welcomed our first child, Olivia. I was spread far too thin, and she was there to pick up my slack. Sarah was also instrumental in the initial editing process. I'm fortunate to have married a high school English teacher.
I'm very proud of my family and friends, and they mean a great deal to me. I wish that everyone had a family like mine.

The team at Channel V Books has been amazing. Erin Ferretti Slattery, Gretel Going, Kate Fleming, Genna Mazor and Cesar Cruz are all on their way to sainthood for their tireless work on this book.

And finally, I would like to acknowledge you. You are taking the time to better your financial life, and that makes me excited. Anyone can be a financial success, but not everyone has the fortitude to start the process. Congratulations!

About the Author

Peter Dunn realized that he wanted to deal with money when he was in his sixth-grade math class. The teacher gave the class a stock-market project, and Pete was hooked.

Like many young people, Pete went through a nasty day trading habit in college. He did well, but his nerves took a beating. Two years into the real world, Pete started a financial advising company, Advanced Planning Solutions.

Pete wrote his first book, *What Your Dad Never Taught You About Budgeting*, in 2006 and is the host of the popular radio show *Skills Your Dad Never Taught You* on News Talk 1430 (WXNT). He's also the mastermind behind WISH-TV8's *60 Days to Change* and appears regularly on FOX News and *Studio B with Shepard Smith*. When not wrapped up in writing or dabbling in broadcast, Pete moonlights as "Pete the Planner," his super-saving radio alter ego.

Pete was named one of "Indy's Best and Brightest" in finance in 2007 and media in 2009 by KPMG, and was declared one of *NUVO* magazine's "30 under 30 to Watch in the Arts" for comedy. *60 Days to Change* is his second book.

Pete currently lives in Carmel, Indiana, with his wife, Sarah, and his daughter, Olivia.

Index